T0294035

ASIAN HERBAL SOUPS
& ONE-POT MEALS

Terry Tan

Marshall Cavendish
Cuisine

First published as Cooking with Chinese Herbs, 1983
© 2004 Marshall Cavendish International (Asia) Private Limited

This new edition 2015

Published by Marshall Cavendish Cuisine
An imprint of Marshall Cavendish International

All rights reserved

No part of this publication may be reproduced, stored in a retrieval system or transmitted,
in any form or by any means, electronic, mechanical, photocopying, recording or otherwise,
without the prior permission of the copyright owner. Request for permission should be addressed
to the Publisher, Marshall Cavendish International (Asia) Private Limited,
1 New Industrial Road, Singapore 536196.
Tel: (65) 6213 9300, Fax: (65) 6285 4871. E-mail: genref@sg.marshallcavendish.com
Online bookstore: http://www.marshallcavendish.com/genref

Limits of Liability/Disclaimer of Warranty: The Author and Publisher of this book have used their best efforts
in preparing this book. The Publisher makes no representation or warranties with respect to the contents
of this book and is not responsible for the outcome of any recipe in this book. While the Publisher has
reviewed each recipe carefully, the reader may not always achieve the results desired due to variations
in ingredients, cooking temperatures and individual cooking abilities. The Publisher shall in no event
be liable for any loss of profit or any other commercial damage, including but not limited to special,
incidental, consequential, or other damages.

Other Marshall Cavendish Offices:
Marshall Cavendish Corporation. 99 White Plains Road, Tarrytown NY 10591-9001, USA •
Marshall Cavendish International (Thailand) Co Ltd. 253 Asoke, 12th Flr, Sukhumvit 21 Road, Klongtoey
Nua, Wattana, Bangkok 10110, Thailand • Marshall Cavendish (Malaysia) Sdn Bhd, Times Subang, Lot 46,
Subang Hi-Tech Industrial Park, Batu Tiga, 40000 Shah Alam, Selangor Darul Ehsan, Malaysia

Marshall Cavendish is a trademark of Times Publishing Limited
National Library Board (Singapore) Cataloguing in Publication Data

Tan, Terry, author.
Asian herbal soups & one-pot meals / Terry Tan. – Singapore : Marshall Cavendish Cuisine, 2015
pages cm
ISBN : 978-981-4561-60-0 (paperback)

1. Soups – Asia. 2. Cooking (Herbs) – Asia. I. Title.

TX757
641.813095 -- dc23   OCN 886465966

Printed in Singapore by Colourscan Print Co Pte Ltd

ASIAN HERBAL SOUPS & ONE-POT MEALS

Acknowledgements

The author wishes to thank Christopher Tan for his cooking and styling efforts and Dr. Geng Yu Ling for her recipes and professional input as a Traditional Chinese Medicine (TCM) practitioner.

Contents

Preface

For thousands of years, within the pantheon of revered Chinese culinary practices, the school of herbal cooking has always been cherished for its restorative elements and hearty prescription for every human ill. Soups, stews and teas that have curative promise are legion and deemed to effectively restore *Qi* and to correct any bodily imbalance. The founding tenet of Traditional Chinese Medicine (TCM), under which herbal brews are a respected and revered school, points to this very imbalance that causes many human ills. Herbal foods may be regarded as being primarily preventative, underscoring the adage "prevention is better then cure". It is by this dictum that we should regard herbal cooking — as an ancient and time-honoured branch of Chinese cuisine that fathoms the efficacy of a multitude of herbs, barks, roots, nuts and seeds when paired with meat, poultry, vegetables or seafood. Even for skeptics chary of this claim, there is the undeniable fact of sheer tastiness.

A distinction is to be made between specific medicinal preparations in TCM and herbal ones that transform everyday dishes into powerhouses of sustenance. While the former can be distasteful to those unused to strong and even foul flavours, the range of herbs used in this book are generally milder and used in judicious tandem with familiar meats and vegetables.

In this school of cooking, little is added by way of artificial flavourings as the intention is to let the herbs do the work. Those unaccustomed to such dishes may initially find them strange, but when the healthy promise behind each blend has been felt, a willing acceptance will follow. Rest assured that there are no dire consequences to be feared in enjoying duck with bitter apricot kernels; chicken with Chinese wolfberries; or pork with Chinese angelica, or *dang gui* as it is better known in Mandarin. With this book, it will be possible for even the most diffident of cooks to produce a wide spectrum of delicious and wholesome dishes, not to mention there is much room for adaptation and innovation even within the fairly rigid framework that governs herbal mixes. Regard this book as a vital entry to your library of good eating tomes, adding to the richness that is Chinese cuisine. It will certainly enrich your table, whatever the efficacious promise.

Introduction

Setting out to write this book proved a formidable challenge. Up until that point, the little I knew about herbal mixes was mostly limited to what my parents once coaxed me to drink or eat in a bid to restore my balance of Yin and Yang (see *Yin-Yang Philosophy and Food*). The prospect of rooting out recipes from old aunts, herbalists, friends and seasoned practitioners of herbal cooking was excitingly delicious, if uphill some of the way. Some herbalists to whom I spoke were not exactly forthcoming, although many others were. Over many months, I learnt to appreciate the profound and tasty promise of such dishes as chicken with ginseng soup; braised duck with lotus seeds; and mutton with the somewhat mystical cordyceps (*dong chong xia cao*). That said, there is really no deep mystery about Chinese herbal cooking. One need only have faith in an ancient discipline that millions of Chinese already subscribe to with fervour.

In revamping my original publication, I have had the distinct advantage of receiving advice from Dr. Geng Yu Ling (M.Sc.), a TCM practitioner and herbalist registered with the TCM Association (UK) and based in London for the past eight years. Dr. Geng is also a medical doctor and specialist in internal medicine. She sought TCM training in Beijing University after completing her clinical studies in her hometown of Hubei. I had first seen Dr. Geng for a pesky bladder problem. Despite several specialists in London, I was still like a leaky bucket and had been for more than two decades. She diagnosed my problem as "dysfunctional kidneys" and prescribed a course of treatment involving cordyceps. Within two months, my problem vanished. I have always had faith in TCM and this served only to reinforce it. Dr. Geng has also been instrumental in providing much background information on every dish in this book. From her, I have learnt so much more about herbalism.

The Semantics of Herbal Cooking

The Chinese herbal ingredients used in this book are without overpowering odours that characterise many blends and poultices often slapped on festering sores. Neither are they evil-smelling brews from a fumy cauldron frothing with medicinal mixes. The world and a half today have come to realise that many of the thousands of dried barks, seeds, nuts and herbs traditionally used in TCM treatment also lend themselves to a range of everyday dishes that are the better for their inclusion.

It is not easy for those uninitiated to fully learn all the health implications in each blend of herbs, complex or simple, as most of such knowledge has been handed down by word of mouth over centuries. What is of paramount importance, then, is that herbal brews are concocted according to individual body constitutions, as well as physical and emotional states. The TCM practitioner seeks to get at the root of the problem rather than the symptom and believes that there can be no panacea for all ills.

TCM dictates that illnesses can be caused by one factor or a combination of several; externally, these are heat, dampness and dryness, and internally, they encompass more than just physical dysfunction to include the effects of happiness, anger, anxiety, grief, fear and trauma, as well as injuries, minor wounds, and over-indulgence. It is, therefore, wise to avoid foods that are extreme in taste, be they spicy, salty, sweet and etc.

In TCM, individual foods are also believed to have characteristics that affect the human constitution. The list here is long and has been broken down into notes preceding the relevant recipes. Suffice to say, for now, that herbal cooking is classically categorised according to poultry, meat, seafood and vegetable dishes, as well as soups and teas.

Poultry such as duck and goose provide meat that is protein-rich but also overly fatty, and so should be eaten sparingly by people who suffer from obesity, hypertension, and heart or cholesterol problems. Chicken is regarded as neutral in energy and when combined with either 'hot' or 'cold' herbs take on the characteristics of the accompanying herbal blend. Of all the meats used in herbal cooking, mutton or lamb is oft used for its stimulating and strengthening properties. For seafood, fish is rich in protein but many types of shellfish have the added nuisance of being cholesterol-rich and, hence, should be avoided or used judiciously.

In History

The study of herbs goes back some 3,000 years to the second dawn of Chinese civilization, when history was beginning to be chronicled and ancient analects recorded. In those early writings, references were made to cooked herbs, and hundreds believed to have curative and restorative powers were named. It was not until 1518, during the Ming Dynasty, however, that medicinal knowledge accrued from research and experimentation performed in centuries past were compiled into one book, and by one man. Li Shi Zhen spent most of his adult life endeavouring the onerous task of recording the preventative, diagnostic and curative principles of natural medication. His efforts resulted in the first ever encyclopaedia of Chinese herbs — *Ben Cao Gang Mu* or *the Compendium of Materia Medica*. Li's admirable work detailed the use of some 1,800 herbs, roots, barks, seeds, plants and nuts, and remains to this day the guiding light for all Chinese physicians. By the seventeenth century, the learned tome had found its way to Japan via traders and seafarers, and some years later, it was translated into Japanese. To date, it has been translated into languages including German, French, Korean and Russian.

In as early as the Tang Dynasty, a medical training institute known as the Imperial Medical College, the first of its kind, was set up in the Middle Kingdom. Since then, a legion of men and women have been schooled in diagnosis based on the principles of universal balance and the application of herbal medicine for a wide spectrum of human ills.

The Roots of Sustenance

In primitive times, much of rural China lived on the brink of hunger and the populace sought sustenance in any and every way they could. Farming was, at that time, still a millennium away and hunting was a discouraging struggle in Nature's patch. Traditional sources of food were, in their order of importance, plants, animals and what lay beneath the soil.

Through the ensuing centuries, the people learnt to differentiate between edible and poisonous varieties of roots, barks and seeds, but not before Nature's toxic produce claimed many lives. The deaths, while unfortunate, were not in vain as they became invaluable lessons in identifying poisons and, later, antidotes. Thus was born today's daunting legacy of medicinal blends and practice of incorporating herbs into daily meals. Perhaps to say the protracted documentation of Chinese herbs and, in particular, their treatment of maladies grew from knowledge gained in those uncertain and unrecorded times.

In any case, the line between medicinal efficacy and culinary delicacy grew only thinner with time, as the purposes of food, nourishment and curative effect meshed and merged. As Chinese cuisine evolved, herbs became more and more inextricably linked with everyday foods. There is certainly more to the adage "medicine and food come from the same source" than we realise.

Herbal dishes are customarily double-boiled, braised or steamed and rarely, if ever, fried. Fat, in fact, is reduced to a minimum in herbal cooking. There is also a certain clarity of flavours, which is the result of allowing the natural tastes and smells of the chosen ingredients to come through unadulterated and unmasked by a barrage of seasonings. It remains the cornerstone of Chinese herbalism that while a headache can be relieved with an analgesic, it is best remedied by attaining overall, physical well-being through the frequent consumption of this herbal soup or that herbal stew. Herbal cooking is a classic cuisine in its own right, and with increased creativity in the field, the experience of herbal foods will, no doubt, be taken far beyond the sometimes stodgy medicinal realm. In the very least, it will make for tasty, wholesome nutrition and, with help from this book, even fine dining at times.

Yin-yang Philosophy and Food

When interest in Feng Shui swept over parts of the world in recent years, in its shadow resided, more basically, principles of Yin and Yang. Yin-Yang theory has long since informed Chinese thought and beliefs, although some strict modernists will continue to regard it as mystical nonsense. In traditional Chinese culture, everything boils down to the opposing forces of Yin and Yang. The former, in broad strokes, represents the Moon, Earth, female gender and darkness, as well as the negative properties of coldness, passivity and softness. The latter, at the other end of the spectrum, represents the Sun, Heaven, male gender and light, as well as such properties as heat, activity and hardness. The ultimate and deceptively simple objective is to strike a perfect balance between the opposing forces by aiding their mutual interaction. In a crass generalisation, then, a person harbouring elements or a state of 'coldness' can counter the condition by eating 'hot' foods and, likewise, elements of 'heat' can be countered by drinking 'cooling' brews, or brews made from 'cold' herbs.

Creating a blend of herbs that complements everyday ingredients to achieve balanced Yin and Yang is an art a lot more complex than many realise. Good herbalists know not only how to make blends that have all the right herbs in the right proportions, but also how much of meat, poultry, seafood or vegetables to use in relation to each blend. Bearing in mind that the counteracting properties of the herbs have to mesh perfectly not only with one another, but also with those of the common ingredients, and altogether with the body that consumes them to produce the internal, Yin-Yang equilibrium that is so craved.

So pervaded is Chinese food and nutrition by concepts of Yin and Yang, however, that regard for the opposing forces is not limited to the relationship between one's body and the ingestion of categorically 'hot', 'cold' and 'neutral' foods. In fact, the influence of Yin-Yang extends to cooking and the creation of tastes. By the laws of Yin and Yang, the flavour of a dish should be the balanced sum of opposites and no one flavour should be unabashedly forward. It would be nearly impossible now to not mention the universally loved sweet-and-sour formula, arguably the Big Mac of Chinese food in the world. In it, vinegar, which is considered a negative element for its sourness, is countered and harmonised with some sugar. It is this insistence on balance that makes Chinese cuisine what it is — a totally logical school of cooking that encompasses many sub-schools, including herbal cooking.

Although the quest for Yin-Yang equilibrium is a considerable deciding factor in the food choices and eating habits of many Chinese, it is just as often that they select certain foods motivated by little more than symbolic meanings. The Chinese propensity to be influenced by symbolism in all facets of life is notorious, and equally famous is the people's passion for food. Indeed, then, dishes made from ingredients that are rife with symbolic meanings have always held a special fascination. Regardless what the modern Chinese may declare to believe or disbelieve, it is a powerful, if sometimes inexplicable, force that spurs crowds to buy symbolic foods during the festive seasons. Chicken, to illustrate, is almost always featured in festive dishes because it represents the heraldic Phoenix, a symbol of rebirth following its proverbial rise from the ashes. The exchanging of tangerines or Mandarin oranges during the lunar or Chinese New Year is another classic example. In Cantonese, the words for "tangerine" and "gold" sound identical — *kum*. With time, tangerines came to represent "prosperity" given the Chinese penchant for the precious metal. That the pun made sense only in southern China did not stop the practice from being adopted by Chinese elsewhere in China or the world. In the official Chinese tongue of Mandarin, the word for "tangerine" does not sound remotely similar to that for "gold".

Numbers are probably the single largest contributor of symbolic meanings to Chinese dishes, connoting multiple meanings for each dish. The frequent combination of three ingredients in one dish, for example, holds a great more symbolism than meets the eye. The number three has portentous significance

represented visibly by the legendary trio of *Fu Lu Shou* (Prosperity, Happiness and Longevity) for rare is the traditional Chinese household without their statuettes; seasonally by the Three Friends of Winter — bamboo, pine and plum; or ideologically by the Three Celestial Lights — the Sun, Moon and constellation of Stars. Incidentally, even numbers are considered Yang in energy and odd numbers Yin. While a traditional Chinese festival spread featuring pork, chicken, duck and fish has since endeared itself to the hearts of many for reputedly representing the Four Heroes of Chinese mythology, the number five is probably the most significant in relation to TCM. For the TCM practitioner, the Five Elements of Wood, Metal, Water, Fire and Earth are as influential as the forces of Yin and Yang in affecting a person's body and health. Each element is governed by a different set of properties and, in turn, governs a different selection of body parts. Corresponding to Wood, Metal, Water, Fire and Earth, for example, are the liver, spleen, heart, lungs and kidneys, all of which are considered Yin in energy. Thus, the art of the Chinese physician lies in his or her ability to, first, accurately read the warning signs left by the overlapping influences of the Five Elements and of Yin and Yang on a person's body, and then resolve the problems by prescribing a suitably counteracting blend of herbs. If the diagnosis and prescription are accurate, then the body's internal equilibrium, and therefore health, will be restored. Season with *wu xiang fen*, or "five-spice powder" in Mandarin, or drink *wu wei tang*, which is "five-flavoured soup" and a dessert made from longan flesh, barley, gingko nuts, dates and dried persimmon, for humble but meaningful reminders of the Five Elements.

Utensils in Herbal Cooking

It is more than circumstantial that Chinese herbal cooking has for most part of its history been bound by a strict code: that only clay, terra cotta or earthenware pots should be used and metal like aluminum should always be avoided. Some qualification is needed for those antiquated culinary rules, however, simply because the development of science has since thrown up innumerable man-made materials, such as heavy enamel, reinforced alloys and non-stick surfaces, that can be effectively and safely utilised for brewing even the strongest herbs. Use and care of utensils are, therefore, largely governed by common sense, with a little extra from the basic guide we provide here.

UNGLAZED CLAY POTS

Traditional clay pots for herbal and medicinal brews were rotund, rough and unglazed crocks with slender spouts for spill-free pouring. Those designed for large pieces of meat or poultry were wider around the neck and had handles for easy lifting. Though shapes and sizes varied and evolved over the centuries, the material used remains porous clay. Today, clay pots continue to be known as "sand pots" in Cantonese (*sha po*) and Mandarin (*sha guo*) because the clay used to make the pots has been mixed with sand for a gritty texture.

Clay pots with unglazed surfaces need gentle handling for two reasons: they crack easily under intense heat and the porous clay absorbs flavours. Detergents, if used at all to remove stubborn stains and grease, must be rinsed off quickly and thoroughly. Always rinse with clean water, preferably hot or warm so the risk of causing cracks from sudden changes of temperature is minimised. Wipe dry with a clean kitchen towel.

The alternative to not having to remove stubborn grease from a porous clay surface is to keep different pots for different foods. A clay pot used for meats and poultry, for example, should not be used for seafood or vegetables, and one used for herbal teas should never be used for anything else. Be extremely careful not to bang your clay pot against any hard surface as hairline cracks are easily caused and not readily visible. Some stores sell clay pots that are reinforced with wire to prevent them from breaking up.

While clay does not conduct heat as effectively and rapidly as metal, clay pots can still become very hot with prolonged cooking. Always use a wad of cloth or kitchen gloves to handle them. Clay pot lids also have a tendency to go separate ways from their parents. To prevent this, tie one end of a cord around the ring or knob on the lid and the other end to the handle firmly.

Unglazed Clay Pots

GLAZED CLAY POTS

Like their unglazed cousins, these can be used safely on the range, whether gas or electric. Glazed clay pots come in two types: those with only the interior glazed and others that are glazed all over. The latter variety serves no greater purpose except aesthetics as they can go from stove to table. The difference between using glazed and unglazed clay pots does not manifest itself enough for even the sharpest tastebud to detect; the glazing merely reduces the absorption of fats, liquids and flavours by an otherwise porous surface.

Glazed clay surfaces are generally less likely to crack or stain and are easier to wash. Detergent maybe used sparingly but the best way is to use hot water, which removes grease far more effectively than cold. Avoid plunging a hot pot into cold water as the sudden change in temperature might cause it to crack from stress. Also, if you have to store more than one, do not stack them as downward pressure can cause hairline cracks.

DOUBLE-BOILERS

Fundamental to herbal cooking, double-boilers work on the principle of heat diffusion through water. Basically made up of two containers, the rim of the smaller inner one is made to rest on top of that of the larger outer one so that the smaller container is suspended and away from direct heat. To use a double-boiler, fill the void between the base of the smaller container and that of the larger container with some water, then place the entire setup over heat. Steam from the boiling water will envelop the inner container and gently cook the food inside. Double-boilers are also excellent for making custards and a favourite Peranakan or Straits Chinese coconut jam called *kaya*.

The alternative to a double-boiler is a ceramic contraption the Cantonese call *dun chung*. Under the dome-shaped lid is a smaller, flat lid. Food is placed inside the container, and after the two lids have been secured, the *dun chung* is steamed for several hours.

Glazed Clay Pots

Metal Double-boilers

SLOW COOKERS

Also known as crock pots, these are excellent for low-heat simmering over a long period of time. Slow cookers have three main parts: the lid, the pot, and the pot-casing. The pot is mostly made entirely of porcelain, sometimes with heavy bottoms for especially slow diffusion of heat. Some pots have metal outer layers that help to conduct heat more effectively, but the whole point of slow cooking is to do it gently so there is no furious bubbling and much less evaporation. Make sure all leads and sockets are removed before washing and be mindful of what the socket comes into contact with.

METAL UTENSILS

Only utensils made from stainless steel, heavy cast-iron or copper may be used for herbal cooking. These require minimal care and the best cleanser is hot water followed by gentle scrubbing with a soft sponge. Metal scourers should not be used as the scratches they leave on the surface attract food grit and other small particles.

NON-STICK COOKWARE

Probably more than any other kitchen innovation, non-stick cookware, which is sold under many proprietary brands, have freed us from the slavery that is pot scrubbing. Herbs can be quite safely cooked in these as long as there is no danger of unsavoury and potentially toxic chemical reactions; where parts of the non-stick surface has worn off, for example. If this happens, discard them. Non-stick utensils are coated with a special alloy that resists adherence but must be treated with extreme gentleness. Stirring should be performed carefully and never with sharp-edged metal ladles. These days non-stick utensils can be heated without any liquid in them but this is not advisable as intense heat can still cause blistering. In any case, all herbal dishes contain liquid and frying as such is never employed. Use wooden or special heat-proof plastic or rubber spatulas.

Ceramic Double-boilers

Slow Cookers

ENAMEL COOKWARE

Enamel cookware comes in many grades. A thin coating chips easily, while a thick one can last a lifetime if taken care of well. The enamel works much like non-stick alloys and is a perfect surface for herbal dishes as there is minimum sticking and grease washes off easily. Care must be taken not to chip the interior as any exposed metal will rust, which demands that the utensil be discarded.

PRESSURE COOKERS

No other cooking utensil cuts cooking time like pressure cookers, and it is fallacious that food cooked quickly is not as nutritious. In fact, few nutrients are lost since little to no evaporation takes place, and tough cuts of meat take half the time to tenderise. A few fundamentals apply when using pressure cookers, however, and one of which is that liquids must not come up to more than two-thirds the height of the pot as the remaining space will not be large enough to contain the intense pressure that will build up.

Clean a pressure cooker as you would any metal pot, but use a soft brush to clean the pressure gauge to prevent clogging. The safety valve on the lid should be released gently and cleaned of any food particles. To remove stubborn stains from the interior, fill the pot with soapy water and scrub away after an hour or so.

Enamel Cookware

Storing Herbs

All dried herbs, barks, seeds and nuts should be stored in jars with tight-fitting lids. It is not a good idea to use opaque containers as any deterioration would not be immediately noticed. Use clear glass jars instead, but keep them away from strong sunlight. Remember, also, that cooking fumes are easily absorbed by dried herbs, so keep them away from where they are susceptible.

Weights and Measures

Most dried herbs are extremely light and traditional herbalists would use the old-fashioned *daching* or Chinese balance to determine quantities that are too slight for the common scales. Although digital scales are increasingly assuming the role of the *daching* into the twenty-first century, many herbalists continue to rely on a combination of skill and instinct in determining how much of each herb is needed for a given blend. Despite the seeming imprecision, few are known to have rejected the expertise of a herbalist in favour of doing their own measuring and blending of ingredients. As for the volume of liquid that accompanies a herbal blend, the age-old practice of measuring by the number of Chinese soup bowls often still applies. In the pursuit of clarity, however, all liquid measures in this book have been metricised.

The A–Z of Chinese Herbs

The glossary here lists the herbs in their English names, which are accompanied by their Mandarin names in han yu pin yin and phonetically spelt Cantonese names. Refer to the chart at the end of this glossary for the corresponding botanical names, as well as Mandarin names in Chinese characters.

APRICOT KERNELS
(*XING REN/HUNG NGAN*)

Also known as "Chinese almonds", kernels of the Mongolian apricot, are also found in the former Manchuria and the northern Chinese provinces of Hebei, Beijing and Shandong. In Korea, it is used as an expectorant and a remedy for dry throats, lung diseases and laryngitis. In China and Japan, it is regarded as a sedative for respiratory problems, a tonic and remedy for severe colds, asthma, rheumatism, swollen feet and constipation. In Indochina, a special preparation of the smashed fruit is chewed but not swallowed, to protect the bronchial tubes from cold during winter.

Herbal shops stock two types of apricot kernels: *bei xing*, the bitter, northern variety, and *nan xing*, the sweet, southern variety. The former are smaller and rounder than the latter and most Chinese herbalists are likely to identify them as bitter and sweet almonds respectively. Both are usually used at the same time, and in equal proportions.

ASTRALAGUS ROOT
(*HUANG QI/PUK KEI*)

Found in Korea and the northern Chinese provinces of Shanxi and Gansu, the pale yellow roots are believed to be good for the treatment of poor blood circulation and fatigue.

Bitter apricot kernels

Sweet apricot kernels

Astralagus root

BARLEY (*YI MI/YI MAI*)

The kernels of the barley plant, which grows from India to southern China and New Guinea, are separated from their shells and used both as food and medicine throughout Asia. Barley is believed to be especially good for babies and young children when boiled with a small amount of winter melon rind. Barley is also good for the treatment of ailments connected with the lungs, as well as rheumatism, dropsy and even gonorrhea!

BIRD'S NEST (*YAN WO/YEEN WOR*)

Gourmets and other lovers of Chinese cuisine will wax lyrical about bird's nest, but it brings different lumps to different throats. Bird's nests are the dried cups of gelatinous, regurgitated saliva with which swifts line their nests. The substance hardens and holds feathers and twigs together to form cosy cups, in which baby swifts nestle with beaks wide open in perpetual hunger.

The fact that bird's nest can be horrendously expensive probably has everything to do with its inaccessibility. Swifts' nests are found mainly in Southeast Asia and the southern Chinese provincesof Guangdong and Fujian. The nests are usually found inside dark caves along the coasts and tucked deep inside crevices.

Whatever the vicissitudes of clambering up and down steep cliffs on bird's nest gathering missions, the fruits of such nerve-wrecking labour are esteemed by millions of Chinese and thousands more of latter-day bird's nest lovers in the western world. Bird's nest is believed to cleanse the blood of impurities, do wonders for the respiratory system, and also ward off influenza and the common cold. Taking this belief one step further, it is said that one should take it either in the middle of the night or first thing in the morning, or even after waking up from a deep sleep. The reason being that the body is totally relaxed to absorb the optimum benefits from Nature's own food.

Barley

Bird's nest

As a delicacy, bird's nest transcends all social barriers. Humble families will buy a little of it to simmer with not much more than rock sugar and then consume it as a sweet dessert. The more affluent will pay a king's ransom for whole cups of bird's nest and have their cooks prepare dishes of imperial flavour with chicken, duck and other culinary esoterics.

As is the case with Chinese food products such as shark's fin and dried scallops, bird's nest comes in different grades which, of course, correspond with cost. Since it is not an easy task to differentiate between so-so bird's nest and top-grade cups, one has to rely on the dictum "you pays your money and you takes your choice". There is usually little diddling and the more you pay, the better quality you get. As a rule of thumb, bird's nest from China is regarded as superior to that from Indonesia and East Malaysia, and the thicker and denser the strands, the better the bird's nest. At the top of the scale is the precious product called *shuet wor* in Cantonese or "blood nest", which is pale brown in colour and speckled with red — believed to be little blood droplets regurgitated by the swifts.

Though bird's nest usually comes nicely cleaned and somewhat bleached in appearance, purists tend to suspect that chemicals may have been added in the process, which was why so many younger members of families, yours truly included, used to be marshalled to spend hours picking at twiglets, feathers and other grit from bird's nest not thoroughly cleaned.

BUDDHA'S FRUIT (LUO HAN GUO/ LOR HAWN GOR)

Also known as arhat fruit, Buddha's fruit comes from a literal translation: *lor hawn* for "Buddha" and *gor* for "fruit". It is found in Guangxi, Sichuan and Hubei provinces of China. Why it

Buddha's fruit

Chinese angelica

is called after the venerable sage is obscure, but it reflects the Yin-Yang symbolism of roundness. It is about the size and shape of a kiwi fruit, greenish-brown, with a thin shell that crumbles easily. It is good for the treatment of tumours, as well as less serious conditions like boils, piles and cramps.

CHINESE ANGELICA
(DANG GUI/DONG KWAI)

Recognised as one of the most effective herbal ingredient for a whole range of gynaecological ailments, *dang gui*, as it is called in Mandarin, is rarely sold whole. Each piece of the stubby root is divided into three sections, each with its specific strengths. Known to the Chinese as 'head' (top), 'body' (middle), and 'tail' (end), the three sections of the root are always sliced paper thin when sold. The plant is cultivated in the high mountains of western and northwestern China and taken by women after childbirth to alleviate pain, lubricate the intestines and prevent haemorrhage.

CHINESE WOLFBERRIES
(GOU QI ZI/GEI CHI)

These small red berries are from a plant found in East Asia and Inner Mongolia. Both fruit and bark of the plant are used in medicine to improve vision and to adjust renal function. Chinese wolfberries also believed to be remedial for diabetes but paradoxically impart a sweetish flavour to most rich stews and soups. Herbalists sell the berries dried.

CHINESE YAM (SHAN YAO/WAI SAN)

The plant from which these chalk-white slivers are produced grow in Korea and China, and also in the Chinese provinces of Henan and Hunan. They are believed to be a tonic for the kidneys

Chinese wolfberries

Chinese yam

and lungs, and are prescribed for diarrhoea, diabetes and urinary problems. It is sometimes referred to as *huai shan* in Mandarin, which corresponds with the common Cantonese name of *wai san*, because the Huaishan region in China is believed to produce the best of its kind.

CHRYSANTHEMUM (*JU HUA/KOK FA*)

Infusing flower petals in hot water to extract fragrance is by no means an exclusively Chinese practice. Early Europeans were imbibing chamomile, magnolia and camellia teas long before Earl Grey graced the inner sanctums of an English drawing room. The Chinese, however, not only made an art of brewing all manner of drinks from magnolia, chrysanthemum and other more obscure blooms, they also deified some varieties, making the full or partial ingestion of such flowers symbolic gestures.

More than any other, the chrysanthemum rose from relative obscurity to become known as a universal balm believed to be efficacious for a whole host of ailments. These range from a weak liver to poor eyesight, bad circulation, infections, digestive upsets, nervous disorders, menstrual irregularity, greying hair and unhealthy blood.

The plants are in full flower in November; this explains their profusion during the Chinese New Year season in January. The flowering branches are picked, tied into neat bundles, hung upside down and dried in the shade. The dried heads are then cut off, bleached with sulphur gas, put at once into the sunshine and air and shaken in a large sieve so that the heads become rounded.

The two most used species are the *chrysanthemum indicum*, which grows wild in most parts of China except the cold north, and the *chrysanthemum morifolium*, commonly cultivated in pots in Singapore and other parts

Chrysanthemum

of Southeast Asia, as well as in the Chinese provinces of Anhui and Zhejiang.

CODONOPSIS ROOT
(DANG SHEN/DONG SAM)

Two species of the root exist — one is a native of the region consisting of the former Manchuria and the northern China, namely the provinces of Inner Mongolia and Qinghai; while the other originated from Qinghai but has come to be cultivated in the central Chinese provinces of Sichuan and Hubei. The root is generally used as a tonic and stimulant reputedly good for the treatment of gonorrhea, blood circulation and gynaecological diseases. In some parts of Asia, it is widely adopted as a respectable substitute for the more expensive ginseng. Herbal medicine researchers have recorded that the extract of the codonopsis root can increase the number of red corpuscles and reduce the number of leucocytes in the blood. The codonopsis root is sometimes mistakenly identified and believed to be the mid-section of ginseng.

CORDYCEPS (DONG CHONG XIA CAO/TUNG CHUNG CHO)

The cordycep's Mandarin name, *dong chong xia cao*, literally translates into "worms in winter, grass in summer". Indeed, the cordycep begins life as a lowly worm that creeps about in winter, undergoes metamorphosis through spring to become a plant in summer, and dries up to fall like a shrivelled twig in autumn. It is the shrivelled twigs that are collected as cordyceps. They are found mainly in China, specifically in the provinces of Sichuan, Qinghai, Guizhou and Yunnan, and only experts with the well-honed powers of truffle hunters can pinpoint the exact underground lair of hibernation.

Codonopsis root

Cordyceps

The cordycep certainly looks like a mummified creepy-crawly with tiny, black, beady eyes that apparently fill with life when the cordycep is put to the boil. As an ingredient reputedly vital to the well-being of one's physical make-up, the cordycep is believed to rejuvenate and reinstate life's vigour by virtue of its incredible resilience, as well as improve lumbago and general debility.

EUCOMMIA BARK (DU ZHONG/DOU CHONG)

A bark found in the Chinese provinces of Sichuan, Shanxi, Hubei and Henan, it is believed to have a tonic effect on the liver, kidneys, bones and ligaments. It is widely used to treat backache, hypertension and cases of threatened miscarriage.

The bark is peeled in spring and early summer but the tree is never girdled because that would kill it. The pieces of bark are then folded with the inner surfaces together, tied with rice straw and left to 'sweat' for a week. When the inner surfaces are brownish-black, the bark is untied, flattened and dried in the sun. Silver-white threads are revealed when the coarse outer part is scraped off or when the bark is cracked. The extract obtained from pounding the bark, when consumed with wine or pork, is believed to be good for the liver, kidneys and spleen. It is also believed to be something of an aphrodisiac. Eucommia bark is always used in a mixture, and never by itself.

EURYALE SEEDS (QIAN SHI/SEE SAT)

These come from a plant that is cultivated in India, China and Japan. Although literature indicates that all parts of the plant are considered to be tonic and astringent, only the seeds are used. Hard, brown, and looking rather like barley grains, euryale seeds take on a flower-like shape

Eucommia bark

Euryale seeds

when boiled. Believed to be good for diseases of the spleen and the treatment of gonorrhea, the seeds are generally served in the form of a sweet that also features longans.

FOXGLOVE ROOT (TREATED) (*SHOU DI HUANG/SOK DEI*)

Foxglove root comes in two varieties: treated and untreated. The Mandarin and Cantonese names of the treated variety literally translates into "cooked earth", and pieces of the root are rather nondescript in appearance: black and hardened clumps. The plant is grown in northern and northwestern China, and it is the tuberous root or rhizome that is used. In its fresh and untreated form, the root is called *sheng di huang* in Mandarin or *sang dei* in Cantonese, both of which translate into "raw earth". To 'cook' the earth, as it were, pieces of the root are dried in a kiln. Foxglove root is believed to be good for the treatment of cough, headache, vertigo, low blood pressure, backache, threatened miscarriage, inflamed eyes and anaemia, as well as disorders of the kidneys and lungs.

GINGKO NUTS (*BAI GUO/BAK GOR*)

Smooth ivory shells enclosing nuggets of buttery and bitter-sweet flavour, gingko nuts are veritable culinary chameleons. They have an elusive quality about them, a taste that is at once mysterious and yet familiar, rather like perfumed almonds with a slightly bitter aftertaste. They are native to Japan and in the Chinese provinces of Guangxi, Sichuan and Henan.

Gingko nuts are good for asthma, coughs, gynaecological problems, bladder ailments and urinary disorders. An extract of the fruit is supposed to have a strongly deterrent effect on the growth of bacteria causing tuberculosis. Young fruits with their fleshy green outer portion

Foxglove root (treated)

Gingko nuts

are soaked in rapeseed oil and then consumed as a remedy for tuberculosis.

The nuts are sold shelled and unshelled. Unshelled nuts keep well for up to a few months before they become susceptible to a weevil that reduces each nut to pale dust. Shelled nuts can be refrigerated and kept up to a few weeks. To prepare unshelled nuts, give each a sharp tap on the tapered edge with a small hammer or similarly heavy object. Be careful not to use too much force as the soft nut inside can end up bruised or worse, broken.

Once cracked, soak or boil for a few minutes until the brown skin, which is slightly caustic, can be rubbed off easily.

Preparation does not end with cleaned, shelled nuts, even if you have been lucky enough to find them in the supermarket, there is still the fiddly chore of removing the bitter cores that are as fine as needles. To remove cores, push a fine toothpick or skewer through each nut, from the base right through to the other, tapered end. Thus prepared, cook as you would any vegetable.

GINSENG

This strange-looking root has been held in the highest regard by the Chinese and other Asians for hundreds of years. In the world of medicinal herbs, no other product quite matches its formidable reputation for restorative powers, a point that seems to draw more believers than skeptics. In the very least, it is something of an enigma for sheer price alone. You can buy ginseng for a few dollars a root or you could fork out $60,000 for another not much different looking. Such is the mystique of ginseng and its alleged curative powers. How ginseng came to earn and keep its reputation (and price tag) has more versions than the root has secondary

Chinese ginseng

Korean ginseng

roots. The most interesting account, by far, tells of an old Chinese farmer who was at death's door one cold winter night, drank a brew of ginseng and recovered almost instantly to till for a good many more years. The farmer is believed to have drunk the most powerful ginseng of all, reputedly found only in northern China.

Into the twenty-first century, ginseng is widely accepted as belonging to one of three main types — Chinese ginseng (*ren shen/yan sam*); American ginseng (*yang shen/yong sam*); and Korean ginseng (*gao li shen/go lai sam*). American ginseng is sometimes also known as the 'flower-flag' ginseng (*hua qi shen/fa kei sam*) because Chinese of the past likened the numerous stars on the American flag to flowers. Despite what the traditionalists seek to uphold, it is safe to say today that no one type of ginseng is necessarily better than the other. Within each type of ginseng, however, are many grades, and

it is the grade of the ginseng that matters more. Also, the name of the root no longer indicates the geographical origins of the root, but only its species. The lucrative promise of the revered root has spurred growers around the world to try their hand at cultivating any faintly profitable species of ginseng. China, to that end, is the world's largest exporter of American ginseng. Far less important than where the root comes from is how it came to be; wild ginseng is always infinitely more valuable than its farmed counterpart.

Much research has been done on the most famous of Chinese herbs in an effort to discover the secrets that reside within. Since the mid-twentieth century, the root has been thoroughly examined and several physiologically active substances have been isolated — in particular *panaxin* which increases muscular tone; *panax acid* which improves metabolism and the vascular system; *panaquilon* which influences

American ginseng

the endocrine system; *panacen* which stimulates the nerve centres; and *ginsenin* which is supposed to be beneficial for diabetes sufferers — thereby lending some strength to the once disputed beliefs that ginseng invigorates and also encourages healing processes in the body after illness, but perhaps not to the degree of reviving a near dying man, as it reputedly did the farmer.

HASMA (*XUE GE/SHUET KUP*)

Hasma refers to the glands of northern snow frogs that are dried and then sold in the form of brown, crumb-like bits. The crumbs must be soaked in water to soften before use and turn into white, cotton-like clumps with soaking.

HYACINTH BEANS (*BIAN DOU/BEEN DAU*)

Also known as the Egyptian kidney bean, the hyacinth bean has a far less exotic name in Mandarin — *bian dou*, which literally means "flat bean". Widely cultivated in the tropics and sub-tropics, the hyacinth flower is picked just as it is opening, usually in August or September, and then dried in the shade. The bean is sweet and slightly warming, and is prescribed for such discomforts as summer heat disorders, dysentery and bloody stools. On the Malay Peninsula, the Malays sometimes use the leaves to make a poultice for eczema and to treat earache. In Indonesia, water added to the juice from crushed leaves, with a little fennel, is strained and drunk as a 'coolant'.

LILY BULB PETALS (*BAI HE/BAK HUP*)

The bulbs are harvested from July to September, then separated, blanched, dried and bleached in sulphur fumes. Lily bulb petals are believed to be beneficial for an extraordinary range of illnesses,

Hasma

Hyacinth Bean

from pulmonary diseases and ulcers to coughs and dry throats.

LONGAN FLESH
(LONG YAN ROU/LONG NGAN YOK)

Longan, a name derived from its Mandarin and Cantonese counterparts, which literally mean "dragon's eye", is a small, seasonal fruit that comes in bunches. In its fresh form, each longan fruit is about the size of a grape and has a semi-hard, greenish-brown shell. The flesh beneath is sweet, succulent and translucent and holds at its centre a round, dark brown seed; which is how a shelled longan could resemble an eye. A native of East Asia, longan is cultivated in China and parts of Indochina. Herbalists, however, only ever stock dried longans, which come in two forms — in their shells, with stones intact, or ready-shelled as lumps of tightly packed longan flesh. Most herbal shops sell longan flesh that is dark brown in colour. Of late, small, orange-brown Taiwanese dried longans are also being sold. These yield lighter-coloured, more delicately flavoured brews. Much prized in China for its warming and tonic properties, longan flesh is considered to be good for the spleen, heart, kidneys, lungs and mental faculties. It is also prescribed to treat nervous disorders with the powdered kernel used as a styptic.

LOTUS ROOT
(LIAN OU JIE/LEEN NGAU)

This rhizome is from the same plant that gives us lotus seeds and is eaten widely by Asians either fresh or dried. Not strictly a herb, it is nonetheless regarded with a degree of respect within Chinese herbal cooking. The fresh form can be bought covered with mud in wet markets or scrubbed cleaned from supermarkets. Lotus roots look like large tubers, each with numerous

Lily Bulb petals

Longan flesh

holes running down their length and look like perforated pieces of marrow when sliced. Cooked with meat in soups and stews, it is believed to be good for the treatment of diabetes, irregular menstrual flow, constipation and stress. Younger rhizomes contain a starch that is similar to arrowroot and is boiled to a thin porridge to relieve diarrhoea and dysentery.

LOTUS SEEDS (*LIAN ZI/LEEN CHI*)

Lotus seed embryos are believed to be useful in promoting sleep, blood circulation and virility. Traditionally, lotus seeds were sold only by Chinese medicinal shops because they were regarded more as a dried herb than a food. Today, more and more supermarkets are selling them prepacked and precooked to take the work out for you.

Preparing dried lotus seeds is time-consuming because removing the brown skin that clings to the seed is a fiddly task. Soak dried lotus seeds — 20 should suffice for one portion — in plenty of water for at least half an hour before rubbing off brown skins. Alternatively, boil the seeds to shorten preparation time, but allow to cool before gently removing skins so as not to bruise the seeds. It is also natural for the seeds to separate into halves when soaked or boiled. If the seeds used still have their cores — green bits about the size of a grain of rice — remove them as they are bitter in taste. To remove the core of a lotus seed that has not split, push a fine toothpick or cocktail stick through the base of the seed through to the tapered top. Once skinned and cored, wash and drain seeds, then set aside to be added to the pot for simmering, braising or boiling as needed.

Because lotus seeds absorb the predominant flavour in a dish, they taste quite different when cooked with rock sugar or as part of stuffing in

Lotus seeds

Notoginseng root

a duck. Cooked lotus seeds have a texture not unlike boiled chestnuts, only more delicate.

Dried lotus seeds keep indefinitely when stored in an airtight tin free of moisture. Precooked lotus seeds can be refrigerated up to a few days or frozen up to a week. Seeds that have been frozen for more than a couple of days, however, will lose some flavour upon thawing.

NOTOGINSENG ROOT
(TIAN QI/TEEN CHAT)

This is a pebble-like root with faint white specks and is known for its properties in the treatment of internal injuries.

RED DATES (HONG ZAO/HUNG CHO)

Not to be confused with the Mediterranean variety, red dates should be about the size of grapes or smaller, dark maroon in colour and,

when dried, very wrinkled in appearance, almost like small, gnarled prunes. They are recommended for the restoration of vigour and vitality. Chinese honeyed dates (*mi zao/mutt cho*) are generally larger and much sweeter because of their honey coating.

RUE (CHOU CAO/CHOW CHO)

This bitter, fern-like plant, good for cooling down 'hot' body systems, was once only sold by Chinatown vendors specialising in fresh herbs for the brewing of 'cooling' drinks (*liang cha/ leong cha*). Today, just about all herbalists stock dried rue, but drying considerably blunts the plant's uniquely pungent aroma — its name means "stinky grass" in Mandarin and Cantonese. Cooking the fresh herb tames its bitterness. Curiously, when added to sweet bean dessert soups, rue imparts to them a peachy, stone-fruit scent.

Red dates

Chinese honeyed dates

Rue

SOLOMON'S SEAL
(*YU ZHU/YOK CHOK*)

These slivers of yellowish root are good for the treatment of ailments related to the pancreas, lungs and throat. Some also attribute it with aphrodisiac properties.

STERCULIA (BOAT) SEEDS
(*PANG DA HAI/DAI HAU LAM*)

The seed, despite its name, is a kind of fruit and usually found dried, and it expands at an alarming rate when soaked in water. For a chuckle, the seed's Cantonese name means the "olive with the big mouth"; its Malay name, *buah kembang sa mangkok*, means the "fruit that becomes a bowl"; and its Mandarin name beats the others for sheer boldness — *pang da hai* literally translates into the "fat big ocean". What other humble food item could provoke such bizarrely amusing descriptions? As a matter of taste, however, it is rather like white fungus — delicate verging on bland. Nevertheless, take its name literally for it really expands like a blimp gone out of control!

TANGERINE PEEL (*CHEN PI/CHAN PEI*)

The Chinese have been using citrus peel as a herb for centuries, with that of the tangerine being the most widely consumed because of the relative ease in obtaining them. Tangerines in China are mostly cultivated in the provinces of Sichuan and Fujian. Citrus peel, whether lime, lemon, pomelo, tangerine or kumquat, is never discarded but carefully spread out on trays and put out to dry in the sun, sometimes for months. Soups and drinks infused with the essence of tangerine peel are believed to be good for such ailments as coughs, colds, and dyspepsia. In cooking, the tangerine peel essentially gives a zesty kick to soups and stews and a strong lemony flavour that counteracts oil. Adding a piece of tangerine peel to a duck stew, for example, provides a nice foil for greasiness.

Solomon's seal

Sterculia (boat) seeds

Fresh rind is also used in ointments applied to acne and eczema. Some citric juices may be employed as a gargle for sore, inflamed or suppurated throats, and an antiseptic to dress and clean wounds.

WHITE FUNGUS
(BAI MU ER/SHUET YI)

White fungus is the more common name for white tremella mushroom. Aside from colour, it is similar in form to black fungus, which is also known as wood ear fungus (hei mu er/mok yi). Despite its name, cloud ear fungus (yun er/wun yi) looks more like black or wood ear fungus, but is smaller in size and more delicate in taste. White fungus is also known as silver ear fungus (yin er/ngan yi) or snow fungus (xue er/shuet yi) and is sometimes used as a cheap substitute for the more expensive hasma (xue ge/shuet kup). Herbalists sell white fungus dried, and the hard pieces are yellowish-brown in colour. The fungus regains its white colour when soaked in water to soften before use.

WINTER MELON
(DONG GUA/TUNG KWA)

Winter melon rind, dried and sugared, is a popular traditional sweet in some cultures and is probably the most widely known form of the melon, which is a native of tropical Asia and widely grown in many countries. In China, the seeds, rind, pulp and juice of the melon are all regarded as medicinal, with each part believed to be diuretic. Winter melon seeds have also been used as a mild laxative and tonic for the treatment of haemorrhoids, intestinal inflammation, urinary and kidney diseases, diabetes, dropsy and (yet again) gonorrhea! Ashes of the rind is administered to cases of painful wounds and the pulp, when boiled with rock sugar, is believed to be exceptionally 'cooling'.

Tangerine peel

Soaked white fungus

Dried white fungus

Chinese Herbs (Chart and pictorial captions)

Common English	Pinyin	Cantonese	Botanical
Apricot kernel (sweet)	Nan xing 南杏	Nam hung	Prunus armeniaca semen
Apricot kernel (bitter)	Bei xing 北杏	Puk hung	Prunus armeniaca semen
Astragalus root	Huang qi 黄耆	Puk kei	Astragalus membranaceus radix
Barley (kernel)	Yi mi 薏米	Yi mai	Coix lachryma jobi semen
Buddha's fruit	Luo han guo 罗汉果	Lor hawn gor	Momordica grosvenor fructus
Chinese angelica	Dang gui 当归	Dong kwai	Angelica sinensis, cogau radicis
Chinese wolfberry	Gou qi zi 枸杞子	Gei chi	Lycium barbarum fructus
Chinese yam	Shan yao 山药	Wai san	Dioscorea opposita radix
Chrysanthemum	Ju hua 菊花	Kok fa	Chrysanthemum morifolium flos
Codonopsis root	Dang shen 党参	Dong sam	Codonopsis pilosula, radix
Cordyceps	Dong chong xia cao 冬虫夏草	Tung chong cho	Cordyceps sinensis
Eucommia bark	Du zhong 杜仲	Dou chong	Eucommia ulmoides cortex
Euryale seed	Qian shi 芡实	See sat	Euryale ferox semen
Falsestarwort root	Tai zi shen 太子参	Tai chi sam	Pseudostallaria hetrophylla radix
Foxglove root	Di huang 地黄	Tei wang	Rehmannia glutinosa radix conquita
Gingko nut	Bai guo 白果	Bak gor	Gingko bilobae semen

Ginseng (Chinese)	Ren shen 人参	Yan sam	Panax ginseng
Ginseng (American)	Yang shen 花旗参	Yong sam	Panax quinquefolium
Ginseng (Korean)	Gao li shen 高丽参	Go lai sam	Panax ginseng
Hyacinth seed	Bian dou 扁豆	Been dau	Dolichoris lablab semen
Lily bulb petals	Bai he 百合	Bak hup	Lilium brownii bulbus
Lilyturf root	Mai dong 麦冬	Mak tung	Ophiopogonis japonicum tuber
Longan flesh	Long yan rou 龙眼肉	Long ngan yok	Euphoris longana arillus
Lotus root	Lian ou jie 莲藕节	Leen ngau	Nelumbo nucifera gaertn.
Lotus seed	Lian zi 莲子	Leen chi	Nelumbinis nucifera semen
Notoginseng root	Tian qi 田七	Teen chat	Panax notoginseng radix
Persimmon	Shi bing 帘饼	Chi bang	Diospyros kaki calyx
Rue	Chou cao 臭草	Chow cho	Rutae folium, herba
Solomon's seal	Yu zhu 玉竹	Yok chok	Polygonatum odoratum rhizoma
Sterculia (boat) seed	Pang da hai 胖大海	Dai hau lam	Sterculia scaphigera semen
Tangerine peel	Chen pi 陈皮	Chan pei	Citrus reticulata pericarpium
Winter melon	Dong gua 冬瓜	Tung kwa	Benincasa hispida
White fungus	Bai mu er 白木耳	Shuet yi	Tremella fuciformis fructificatio

Important Note

All dried herbs should be gently rinsed with water before being placed into the chosen cooking vessel; this prevents them from charring if they settle at the bottom. Before serving each dish, all herbs can be discarded, if so wished, as they would have amply served their purpose and been extracted of all their goodness during the cooking. Please note also that all salt quantities are suggested amounts that you should adjust to your personal taste; many people prefer to let the herbs' natural sweetness or pungency take centre stage.

Sweet Treats

Some Chinese have the habit of preceding a meal with a sweet soup or drink, while others prefer to serve sweet, between-meal snacks. Sweet soups and drinks usually contain a marrow of some kind, watercress, lotus seeds, gingko nuts, dates and one of the milder Chinese herbs. It might seem a little confusing, too, why a distinction should exist between a sweet soup and a sweet drink when they appear so similar. There is only one explanation for this — tradition. The soups in question have always been served as part of a meal and the drinks outside mealtimes as sweet indulgence. As such, do not be overly bothered by the classifications herein. Suffice to know that rock sugar is the key ingredient in the following recipes.

Lotus Seeds with Hard-boiled Eggs Cooking time: 1 hour • Serves 4-6

This is a 'cooling' brew that is often served as a pick-me-up, and the hard-boiled eggs give it extra substance.

Dried lotus seeds 200 g
Water 2 litres
Eggs 4–6
Rock sugar 200 g

Time-saver
To avoid the hassle of preparing dried lotus seeds, substitute with 250 g precooked lotus seeds.

- Wash and drain precooked lotus seeds.
- Bring water to the boil. Add rock sugar. When sugar has completely dissolved, add lotus seeds. Simmer for 20 minutes or until lotus seeds are soft.
- Meanwhile, prepare hard-boiled eggs as advised.

1. Soak lotus seeds in plenty of water for 30 minutes or boil for 5 minutes. If boiled, allow seeds to cool before rubbing off brown skins if still attached. Split each lotus seed in two. Remove green core if still attached.
2. Bring water to the boil. Add lotus seeds. Simmer for at least 45 minutes.
3. Meanwhile, prepare hard-boiled eggs. To prevent eggs from cracking before they harden, immerse them in a pot of cold water and bring to the boil slowly. Simmer for 8 minutes, then remove to cool. Do not attempt to shell eggs when they are still hot as the shell will not come away cleanly.
4. When lotus seeds are soft enough (taste one to test), add rock sugar and eggs. Heat for 5 minutes more to allow eggs to absorb liquid.

Cooking Know-how
Some brands of rock sugar come with a little grit, so you will need to strain the liquid after the rock sugar has melted for clarity. For added fragrance, tie two screwpine (*pandan*) leaves into a knot and add to the pot when simmering.

Lotus Seeds and Solomon's Seal with Eggs
Cooking time: 45 minutes • Serves 4-6

This recipe is a variation of the preceding one, with Solomon's seal added for aiding pancreatic functions and extra nourishment.

Precooked lotus seeds 200 g
Solomon's seal (*yu zhu/ yok chok*) 15 g, rinsed
Rock sugar 150 g
Water 2 litres
Hard-boiled eggs 4, shelled

1. Except eggs, combine all other ingredients in a pot. Simmer for 40 minutes.
2. Add shelled eggs in the last 5 minutes of simmering. Serve hot.

Cooking Know-how
If you want hard-boiled eggs that are well-shaped and have cooked yolks that are not askew, do not let eggs remain in one position as they cook. Instead, use a metal spoon to turn them around once or twice. This may be important to you if you plan to serve hard-boiled eggs cut up.

Opposite: Lotus Seeds with Hard-boiled Eggs.

Lotus Seeds and Chinese Yam Cooking time: 45 minutes • Serves 4

Lotus seeds are 'neutral' in energy and when combined with Chinese yam, helps to regulate kidney functions.

Precooked lotus seeds
40, washed and drained
Chinese yam (*shan yao/ wai san*) 20 g, rinsed
Rock sugar 150 g
Water 1.5 litres

1. Combine all ingredients in a pot. Simmer over low heat for 20 minutes.

2. Strain if necessary. Reheat to serve warm. Refrigerate for 30 minutes to serve cold.

Cooking Know-how

Some brands of rock sugar come with a little grit, so you will need to strain the liquid after the rock sugar has melted for clarity. For added fragrance, tie two screwpine (*pandan*) leaves into a knot and add to the pot when simmering.

Lotus Seeds and Gingko Nuts Cooking time: 45 minutes • Serves 4

This is an ultra-simple and yet incredibly effective 'cooling' brew.

Water 2 litres
Dried gingko nuts 40–50, soaked in water for at least a few hours or preferably overnight
Precooked lotus seeds 250 g
Rock sugar 150 g

1. Bring water to the boil. Add gingko nuts. Simmer for 30 minutes.

2. Add lotus seeds and rock sugar. Simmer for 15–20 minutes more, depending on the degree of softness you like for your lotus seeds and gingko nuts. Serve hot or cold.

Lotus Seeds and Gingko Nuts with Sterculia Seed
Cooking time: 1 hour • Serves 4

This is an ultra-simple and yet incredibly effective 'cooling' brew.

Sterculia seed (*pang da hai/dai hau lam*) 1
Dried gingko nuts 40–50, soaked in water for at least a few hours or preferably overnight
Precooked lotus seeds 250 g
Water 2 litres
Rock sugar 150 g

1. Peel sterculia seed. Soak in plenty of cold water. Expansion begins after about 5 minutes. Remove all traces of peel and vein-like strands. Wash to remove fine grit. Set aside. Sterculia flesh does not need to be cooked.

2. Bring gingko nuts, lotus seeds and water to the boil. Simmer over low heat for 20 minutes. When they are soft, add rock sugar. Simmer for 10–15 minutes more. When rock sugar has completely dissolved, remove from heat.

3. Add as much sterculia flesh as required for each serving. Serve hot or cold.

Variations on a Five-flavoured Theme

The classic five-flavoured soup — barley, gingko nuts, lotus seeds, longan flesh and dried persimmon — is not an inflexible recipe. In fact, it varies slightly from dialect group to dialect group within the Chinese community, incorporating such ingredients as white tremella mushroom (bai mu er/shuet yi), more commonly known as white fungus; dried tangerine peel; sweet potatoes; agar-agar; red (adzuki) beans and even bird's nest. The list below draws together the key ingredients of the different versions of the five-flavoured soup. Exercise your culinary imagination and titillate the taste buds with permutations of not necessarily five, but two, three, four or even all of the listed ingredients, some of which are not herbs as such but are complementary to herbals blends.

Dried longan flesh 150 g
Dried persimmons 2, thinly sliced
Dried tangerine peel 6 pieces
Sweet potatoes 450 g
Agar-agar 60 g
Red (adzuki) beans 100 g
Bird's nest 30 g

Regardless of what you have chosen to include in your version of the five-flavoured soup, all recipes require a foundation of about 2 litres water, with 150–200 g rock sugar dissolved in it and either lotus seeds or gingko nuts for a basic ingredient. All recipes require an average of 45 minutes of simmering and serve 4–6 people. Find out how to process each of the listed ingredients below.

Dried longan flesh

Wash and remove all grit and impurities before adding to the pot in the last 15 minutes of simmering. Remember that dried longan flesh is already sweet, and thus, the amount of rock sugar otherwise called for by a recipe can be reduced by up to half, depending on your taste.

Dried persimmon

Fresh persimmons are round, fat, orange fruits with soft flesh and large pits. Dried persimmons, however, bear little resemblance to their fresh counterparts. Expect, instead, flattened brown discs, each covered with a thick dusting of white flour. To prepare dried persimmon, remove the hard centre, wash off the floury coating and cut into thin slices before adding to the pot in the last 15 minutes of simmering. It is slightly sweet, so cut down on rock sugar by about 60 g.

Dried tangerine peel

Simply add a few pieces in the last 15 minutes of simmering or at the beginning if you prefer a stronger citric presence. Be careful as too much will render your brew a little bitter.

Sweet potato

Peel and cut 1-cm thick slices. Add slices in the last 15 minutes of simmering. Alternatively, cook slices separately with sugar, at a proportion of 450 g sweet potatoes to 150 g sugar in 1 litre water. If adopting the latter method, drain and dry a little before adding to the main pot in the last 5 minutes of simmering.

Agar-agar

Also referred to as Japanese gelatin, these translucent, raffia-like strands are made from seaweed and sold by most supermarkets. A fuss-free approach is to soak agar-agar for a few minutes, cut the softened strands into short lengths and then add to the pot in the last 2–3 minutes of cooking. Alternatively, boil about 700 ml water, add 30 g agar-agar strips and 100 g sugar, and cook for about 15 minutes until both are dissolved. Strain through a fine sieve and pour into a mould to set. When set, cut into fine shreds and add to individual bowls as required with other ingredients.

Red (adzuki) beans

Wash and boil about 100 g red beans for 30 minutes or until just cooked, but not mushy. Add to individual bowls as above.

Bird's nest

This ingredient increases the cooking time to at least 1 hour, and if it is being cooked directly from its dried state, it has to be added at the beginning together with such ingredients as gingko nuts or barley.

Gingko Nuts and Barley Cooking time: 1 hour • Serves 4

This 'cooling' brew is known to offset the detrimental effects of having eaten too many 'hot' foods. In TCM, gingko nuts are believed to strengthen the bladder and address related ailments. This was, in fact, the very reason that prompted my mother to cram handfuls of gingko nuts down my throat every week as a child. Today, some five decades later, I make it a point to eat gingko nuts whenever I feel the internal waterworks, as it were, not operating properly.

Dried gingko nuts 40–50, soaked in water for at least a few hours or preferably overnight
Barley 150 g
Water 2 litres
Screwpine (*pandan*) **leaves** (**optional**) 1–2, washed and tied into a knot
Rock sugar 150 g

1. Wash and drain soaked gingko nuts and barley. Bring washed ingredients and water to the boil. Simmer over medium heat for 20 minutes.

2. Add screwpine leaves, if used, for added fragrance. Add rock sugar. Simmer for 40 minutes more.

Cooking Know-how

The state of gingko nuts — whether they are dried or have been soaked, and for how long — just before they are cooked affect the length of cooking time. When done, they should mash easily when pressed with the back of a spoon.

Green Beans and Rue with Tangerine Peel

Cooking time: 45 minutes • Serves 4

This recipe is a variation of the preceding one, with Solomon's seal added for aiding pancreatic functions and extra nourishment.

Water 2 litres
Green beans 250 g, thoroughly washed and drained
Rue (*chou cao/chow cho*) 10 g, washed and drained
Dried tangerine peel 3 pieces
Rock sugar 150 g

1. Bring water to the boil. Add green beans. Simmer for 30 minutes or until beans are just soft.

2. Add rue and tangerine peel. Simmer for 15 minutes. By now, green beans should be very soft.

3. Add rock sugar and simmer until dissolved. Serve hot or cold.

Opposite: Green Beans and Rue with Tangerine Peel.

Red Beans with Tangerine Peel

Cooking time: 1 hour 15 minutes • Serves 4

Red beans, also known as adzuki or aduki beans, are protein-packed and when combined with tangerine peel, makes a 'warming' drink that helps to dispel phlegm and also aid digestion. Although a decent *hong dou tang*, Mandarin for "red bean soup", can be made with just red beans, rock sugar and water, the tangerine peel adds a subtle zest that goes on to make a tremendous difference. If red beans are unavailable, red kidney beans, which are larger but similar in flavour, can be used as a substitute.

Red (adzuki) beans 250 g
Water 2 litres
Rock sugar 150 g
Dried tangerine peel 4–5 small pieces

1. Wash red beans thoroughly. Remove all impurities and spoilt grains.

2. Bring water to the boil. Add beans. Simmer for 1 hour over medium heat. Stir occasionally to prevent beans from sticking to the base. Add more water if necessary.

3. When beans are soft enough to be mashed, add rock sugar.

4. When sugar has completely dissolved, add tangerine peel. Simmer for 15 minutes more. For a more concentrated citric flavour, add tangerine peel earlier in the cooking process.

Cooking Know-how

For traditional authenticity, remove a few tablespoons of cooked beans, mash with a fork and return to the pot so the liquid becomes a bit murky. This sweet soup is rarely served cold as the mashed beans coagulate with refrigeration.

Red Beans and Lotus Seeds with Tangerine Peel

Cooking time: 1 hour • Serves 4

Lotus seeds and red beans have a certain affinity, and lotus seeds also add crunch and body to the sweet soup. The specified amount of lotus seeds is merely a guideline and less or more may be used as long as the lotus seeds do not exceed the red beans in bulk.

Red (adzuki) beans 50 g, washed and drained

Water 2 litres

Precooked lotus seeds 250 g, washed and drained

Rock sugar 150–200 g

Dried tangerine peel 4 pieces

1. Bring red beans and water to the boil. Simmer for 45 minutes.

2. Add lotus seeds and rock sugar. Simmer for 15 minutes more or until lotus seeds are soft.

3. Add tangerine peel at any point during the simmering, depending on your preference for the degree of citric zest.

4. Remove, mash and return to pot a few Tbsp red beans if desired, but not the lotus seeds.

Cooking Know-how

To test cooked lotus seeds for desired softness, use the back of a spoon to press one seed against the side of the pot. Lotus seeds crumble easily when done.

Red Beans in Coconut Milk with Tangerine Peel

Cooking time: 1 hour • Serves 4

This recipe is arguably a Singaporean or South-east Asian hybrid as coconut is rarely used in traditional Chinese cooking. It is, if you like, a cousin to the Nonya (Straits Chinese) dessert of green (mung) beans in coconut milk and is lovely chilled. As far as possible, use only freshly squeezed coconut milk as prepacked coconut milk or cream can be oily.

Red (adzuki) beans 250 g, washed and drained

Water 2 litres

Dried tangerine peel 5 pieces

Rock sugar 200 g

Coconut milk 500 ml

Salt 1/2 tsp

1. Bring red beans and water to the boil. Simmer over low heat for 30 minutes.

2. Add tangerine peel. Simmer for 15 minutes more or until beans are soft. Add rock sugar.

3. When sugar has completely dissolved, add coconut milk. Simmer for no more than 10 minutes or the liquid will become oily.

Cooking Know-how

For purely aesthetic reasons, you could reserve a few tablespoons of coconut milk to drizzle on top just before serving.

Solomon's Seal with Chinese Almonds
Cooking time: 1 hour • Serves 4

Chinese almonds (*xing ren/hung ngan*) are really apricot kernels, and there are two types: sweet and bitter. Both types look much alike, except that the bitter ones are smaller and rounder. The bitter kernels are also rarely used without their sweet counterparts. Combining the two not only acts to 'cool' the body, but also makes a powerful expectorant. Apricot kernels in general are trusted remedies for dry coughs, laryngitis and respiratory ailments.

Solomon's seal (*yu zhu/ yok chok*) 15 g, rinsed and drained

Sweet apricot kernels (*nan xing/nam hung*) 40, rinsed and drained

Bitter apricot kernels (*bei xing/puk hung*) 40, rinsed and drained

Water 2 litres

Rock sugar 150 g

1. Except rock sugar, combine all other ingredients in a pot. Bring to the boil. Simmer over low heat for 40 minutes.

2. Add rock sugar. Simmer for 15 minutes more. Serve warm.

Solomon's Seal with Apricot Kernels and Lotus Seeds
Cooking time: 1 hour • Serves 4

These three ingredients combine particularly well for a subtle flavour.

Solomon's seal (*yu zhu/ yok chok*) 15 g, rinsed

Sweet apricot kernels (*nan xing/nam hung*) 40, rinsed

Water 2 litres

Rock sugar 150 g

Precooked lotus seeds 200 g

1. Bring rinsed ingredients and water to the boil. Simmer for 30 minutes.

2. Add rock sugar. Simmer over medium heat for 10 minutes more.

3. Add lotus seeds. Simmer for 15 minutes or until soft. Serve hot or cold.

Opposite: Solomon's Seal with Chinese Almonds.

Chinese Yam and Solomon's Seal with Longan

Cooking time: 45 minutes • Serves 4

This fragrant drink can take the edge out off an oily meal. Dried longan flesh is 'hot' in energy and is believed to reinforce the blood-building functions of the spleen and heart. It also has appetite-sharpening properties. Usually sold in compressed packs, dried longan flesh is naturally sweet and requires some washing to remove the odd bits of grit. Fresh longans are never a substitute.

Dried longan flesh 200 g

Chinese yam (*shan yao/ wai san*) 15 g, rinsed and drained

Solomon's seal (*yu zhu/ yok chok*) 15 g, rinsed and drained

Rock sugar 100 g

Water 2 litres

1. Wash longan flesh in a bowl of water. At the same time, pry longan pieces loose. Strain in a colander. Be careful not to over-wash as flavour and sweetness will be reduced.

2. Combine all ingredients in a pot. Bring to the boil. Simmer over low heat for about 45 minutes. Longan flesh will colour the liquid a rich brown.

Cooking Know-how

For a change, halve the amount of longan flesh in this recipe and add to it 200 g precooked lotus seeds. First, bring water to the boil. Add rinsed ingredients and longan flesh and simmer for 30 minutes. Then, add lotus seeds and rock sugar and simmer for 15 minutes more. Serve hot.

Chinese Yam and Solomon's Seal Cooking time: 45 minutes • Serves 4

Chinese yam is taken to aid functions of the kidneys and lungs and Solomon's seal for the pancreas, lungs and throat.

Chinese yam (*shan yao/ wai san*) 15 g, rinsed

Solomon's seal (*yu zhu/ yok chok*) 15 g, rinsed

Rock sugar 150 g

Water 1.5 litres

Hard-boiled eggs (optional)

1. Combine all ingredients in a pot. Simmer over low heat for 45 minutes.

2. Hard-boiled eggs may be added to make a more substantial brew.

Cooking Know-how

Add 200 g precooked lotus seeds and 500 ml water to this recipe and simmer for the same duration for a brew the Cantonese describe as *yurn*, which means "to soothe".

Chinese Yam and Solomon's Seal with Apricot Kernels

Cooking time: 45 minutes • Serves 4

This classical quartet makes for a soothing brew that is mildly bitter in flavour. Chinese yam is believed to improve kidney functions.

Chinese yam (*shan yao/ wai san*) 15 g, rinsed

Solomon's seal (*yu zhu/ yok chok*) 15 g, rinsed

Sweet apricot kernels (*nan xing/nam hung*) 40, rinsed

Bitter apricot kernels (*bei xing/puk hung*) 40, rinsed

Water 2 litres

Rock sugar 150 g

1. Except rock sugar, combine all other ingredients in a pot. Bring to the boil. Simmer over low heat for 30–40 minutes.

2. Add rock sugar. Simmer until completely dissolved.

Chinese Yam and Solomon's Seal with Lotus Seeds and Lily Bulb Petals
Cooking time: 1 hour • Serves 4

The infusion of lily bulb petals, a magnolia-like flower, makes this a very fragrant drink. Lily bulb petals are known to address a diverse range of ailments, from pulmonary diseases to ulcers and dry coughs.

Chinese yam (*shan yao/ wai san*) 15 g, rinsed

Solomon's seal (*yu zhu/ yok chok*) 15 g, rinsed

Dried lily bulb petals (*bai he/bak hup*) 20, rinsed

Rock sugar 150 g

Water 2 litres

Precooked lotus seeds 200 g

1. Except lotus seeds, combine all other ingredients in a pot. Bring to the boil. Simmer for 30 minutes.

2. Add lotus seeds. Simmer over low heat for 30 minutes more. Serve hot for optimum fragrance.

Sweet Soups

Among sweet brews that I have learnt to love are those that simmer vegetable marrows long and lovingly with one herb or another and some rock sugar. I did not take kindly to them initially because I had always associated vegetable marrows with savoury dishes. Nevertheless, once I got used to the sweetish flavour of these drinks, which are really more like soups because of their hearty nature, I was forever enamoured.

The Cantonese are particularly fond of using the brown marrow, which they call lo wong kwa, or "old cucumber", and watercress for sweet soups, both of which are reputedly good for dry coughs. The soups are usually served hot but may be served chilled if you so fancy. Do be mindful that red dates impart a considerable amount of sweetness, so rock sugar can be either avoided altogether or reduced to taste.

Walnuts and Red Dates

Cooking time: 1 hour • Serves 4

This blend is said to help prevent common colds, coughs and respiratory problems and also strengthen kidney function and prevent constipation.

Walnuts 150 g, shelled and rinsed
Dried red dates (*hong zao/hung cho*)
    150 g, pitted and rinsed
Water 800 ml
Clear honey 3 Tbsp

1. Except honey, combine all other ingredients in a pot. Bring to the boil. Simmer over low heat for 1 hour.

2. Add honey in the last few minutes. Serve hot.

Brown Marrow and Red Dates Cooking time: 45 minutes • Serves 4

Brown marrow is coarse-skinned and roughly three times the size of a cucumber. In fact, the Cantonese name for the vegetable — *lo wong kwa* — translates into "old cucumber". Its ivory-white flesh is soft, and its creamy pips are mostly edible. Never remove the marrow skin as most of the nutrients lie just under it. The brown marrow lends itself well to either sweet or savoury soups and makes for a very 'cooling' brew.

Brown marrow 1, large (about 400 g)

Dried red dates (*hong zao/hung cho*) 10

Water 3 litres

Rock sugar (optional) 100 g

1. Cut both ends of marrow, about 2 cm from each tip, and discard. Cut remaining marrow into 4-cm wide rings.

2. Remove a little of the core only if the pips are large and hard. Otherwise, leave rings as they are.

3. Wash off any dirt on marrow skin by gently rubbing with hands.

4. Bring red dates and water to the boil. Add marrow rings. Simmer for 45 minutes. If left unstirred, the marrow rings will hold their shape even after being boiled until they are mushy.

5. Add rock sugar only if you like the soup on the sweet side.

Buddha's Fruit and Apricot Kernels Cooking time: 1 hour • Serves 4

Buddha's fruit is believed to be good for the treatment of tumours, boils, piles and cramps. In this brew and others alike, the Buddha's fruit can be either broken up or boiled whole as the brittle skin breaks up eventually anyway.

Buddha's fruit (*luo han guo/lor hawn gor*) 1, whole

Sweet apricot kernels (*nan xing/nam hung*) 20

Bitter apricot kernels (*bei xing/puk hung*) 20

Water 2 litres

Rock sugar 150 g

1. Combine all ingredients in a pot. Simmer for 1 hour. Serve hot.

Buddha's Fruit and Red Dates Cooking time: 45 minutes • Serves 4

This brew is good for cleansing the body, aiding digestion and dispelling constipation.

Buddha's fruit (*luo han guo/lor hawn gor*) 1, whole

Dried red dates (*hong zao/hung cho*) 6

Water 1 litre

Rock sugar 100 g

1. Combine all ingredients in a pot. Simmer for 45 minutes. Serve hot or cold.

Watercress and Red Dates Cooking time: 1 hour • Serves 4

Herbalists recommend this simple sweet soup to be drunk several times a week if you are troubled by a persistent dry cough. The amount of watercress specified is only a guideline; double the amount if a thicker soup is preferred.

Watercress 100 g

Dried red dates (*hong zao/hung cho*) 10

Water 2 litres

1. Combine all ingredients in a pot. Bring to the boil. Simmer over low heat for 1 hour.

2. Top up boiling hot water if liquid lost through evaporation is considerable.

Longan and Red Dates Cooking time: 1 hour • Serves 4

In times past, grandparents received felicitations from their children and grandchildren during the Chinese New Year. Younger members of the family offered their elders, depending on age and status, a cup of bird's nest soup or longan tea and a red date. More affluent families also serve ginseng tea.

Dried longan flesh 150 g

Dried red dates (*hong zao/hung cho*) 40

Water 1.5 litres

Rock sugar 100 g

1. Wash longan flesh to remove grit. Red dates do not need washing, just a wipe with kitchen paper will do.

2. Combine all ingredients in a pot. Simmer for between 45 minutes and 1 hour. Serve hot.

Opposite: Longan and Red Dates.

Watercress with Buddha's Fruit and Apricot Kernels

Cooking time: 1 hour • Serves 4

Watercress is second-richest in iron, after spinach, but is rather neglected in daily cooking. It is delicious raw as part of a salad but remarkably retains its flavour even after prolonged simmering. When preparing watercress for Chinese herbal soups, remove only the roots; do not separate leaves and stems.

Watercress 150 g, washed and roots removed

Buddha's fruit (*luo han guo/lor hawn gor*) 1, whole

Sweet apricot kernels (*nan xing/nam hung*) 20

Bitter apricot kernels (*bei xing/puk hung*) 20

Rock sugar 150 g

Water 2 litres

1. Combine all ingredients in a pot. Simmer for between 45 minutes and 1 hour. Serve hot.

Watercress with Apricot Kernels and Red Dates

Cooking time: 45 minutes • Serves 4

Rich in iron from the watercress, this drink helps to enrich the blood and the apricot kernels help to prevent respiratory problems, colds and constipation.

Watercress 200 g, washed and roots removed

Sweet apricot kernels (*nan xing/nam hung*) 40

Bitter apricot kernels (*bei xing/puk hung*) 40

Dried red dates (*hong zao/hung cho*) 6–8

Water 2 litres

Rock sugar (optional) 100 g

1. Except for rock sugar, combine all other ingredients in a pot. Bring to the boil. Simmer over low heat for 35 minutes.

2. If preferred, add rock sugar or 4–5 more red dates for added sweetness.

Opposite: Watercress with Buddha's Fruit and Apricot Kernels.

Herbal Drinks

You might well ask what the difference is between a sweet herbal soup and a sweet herbal drink. The line of distinction would be that of substance, with the former being heartier and correspondingly heavier, while the latter is lighter and more of a thirst-quencher.

Codonopsis Root and Chrysanthemum Cooking time: 45 minutes • Serves 4

Although codonopsis root (*dang shen/dong sum*) is not strictly of the ginseng family, it can be used for similar purposes — as a 'warming' tonic. People who suffer from high blood pressure, however, are generally advised to avoid ginseng and codonopsis comes under this category as well, although it is significantly less 'hot' than ginseng.

Codonopsis root (*dang shen/dong sum*) 30 g, rinsed
Dried chrysanthemum petals 15 g
Rock sugar 150 g
Water 1 litre

1. Combine all ingredients in a pot. Simmer over low heat for at least 45 minutes.

2. Either strain off pulp or allow to settle before drinking.

Bird's Nest Drink Cooking time: 1-2 hours • Serves 4

Bird's nest is not strictly a medicinal herb but enjoys a good reputation for being a 'warming' food that helps ward off colds and flu-related ailments. Although bird's nest should really be found in the category of double-boiled dishes, it has been included here because bird's nest can also be simmered slowly with rock sugar to make a refreshing drink. There are as many grades of bird's nest as there are feathers on the bird, so the richness of your bird's nest drink essentially depends on the depth of your pocket. For this recipe, the amount of rock sugar can be increased or decreased according to taste.

Bird's nest 60 g
Rock sugar 150 g
Screwpine (*pandan*) leaves 2
Water 1 litre

1. Combine all ingredients in a heavy-bottomed or good enamel pot. Simmer for 1–2 hours. The pot should have a snug-fitting lid to prevent excessive evaporation.

2. Check liquid level occasionally. Add a little water if necessary. Serve warm or thoroughly chilled.

Cooking Know-how

Most herbalists sell bird's nest that is already cleaned. Cleaning unprocessed bird's nest can be tedious and time-consuming. To prepare bird's nest that is in its natural state, first use a pair of previously unused or suitably clean tweezers to pick out impurities like tiny twigs and feathers, then wash several times. The last change of water should be spotlessly clean.

Opposite: Bird's Nest Drink

Bird's Nest and Hasma Cooking time: 1 hour • Serves 4

White on white, these two ingredients combine particularly well for a super-smooth drink that is full of goodness, flavour and texture.

Hasma (*xue ge/shuet kup*) 60 g
Bird's nest 60 g
Rock sugar 150 g
Water 1 litre
Screwpine (*pandan*) **leaves** 3, washed and tied into a knot

1. Soak hasma in plenty of water until completely soft. Snip off any hard bits. Wash and drain well.

2. Combine all ingredients in a pot. Simmer for 1 hour. Serve warm or chilled.

Cooking Know-how

Agar-agar, or Japanese gelatin, can be used either as a substitute for hasma or as a third ingredient for more crunch.

Hasma Drink Cooking time: 45 minutes • Serves 4

This herbal drink will glide down your throat like no other does.

Hasma (*xue ge/shuet kup*) 60 g
Water 1 litre
Rock sugar 150 g

1. Soak hasma in plenty of water until completely soft. Snip off any hard bits. Wash and drain well.

2. Combine all ingredients in a pot. Simmer for 45 minutes or until hasma is almost jellied. Serve warm or cold.

Opposite: Hasma Drink.

Codonopsis and Astragalus Roots Cooking time: 1 hour • Serves 4

Astragalus root at the shops is usually already sliced and packaged. Long, flat and pale-yellow strips, they are said to improve blood circulation and reduce fatigue.

Codonopsis root
(*dang shen/dong sum*)
15 g, rinsed
Astragalus root (*huang qi/*
***puk kei*)** 15 g, rinsed
Rock sugar 100 g
Water 750 ml

1. Combine all ingredients in a pot. Simmer over low heat for about 1 hour. Serve warm.

Codonopsis Root Drink Cooking time: 30-45 minutes • Serves 4

Herbalists often recommend codonopsis root instead of ginseng for children who encounter problems with blood circulation, because ginseng is generally believed to be too potent for children.

Codonopsis root
(*dang shen/dong sum*)
30 g, rinsed
Rock sugar 100 g
Water 1 litre

1. Combine all ingredients in a pot. Simmer over low heat for 30–45 minutes. Drink it warm.

Ginseng and Bird's Nest Cooking time: 1 hour • Serves 4

Whatever grade ginseng you choose, remember that it is a potent herb and no more than a little should be consumed at any one time. Herbalists swear by ginseng for good health, glowing hair and a sparkling disposition.

Bird's nest 60 g
Ginseng 15 g
Rock sugar 150 g
Water 1 litre

1. Combine all ingredients in a pot. Simmer for about 1 hour. Serve hot or cold.

Ginseng Drink Cooking time: 1 hour • Serves 4

Ginseng, much like bird's nest, comes in many grades and the choice of ginseng used for this recipe mostly depends on what you are willing to spend. See glossary at the beginning of this book for an introduction to the various types of ginseng.

Ginseng 15 g
Rock sugar 150 g
Water 1 litre

1. Combine all ingredients in a heavy-bottomed pot; never use aluminium. Also, make sure the pot has a snug-fitting lid to prevent excessive evaporation. Simmer for 1 hour. Ginseng drink should be sipped warm.

Cooking Know-how

Ginseng can be reused a second time to make a weaker but still effective brew.

Herbal Teas

Basic Chinese tea is said to reduce excess 'heat' in the body, quench thirst and soothe minor discomforts or irritations. Depending on the concoction, herbal teas can help clear lungs, dissipate heatiness, kill bacteria, boost immunity, lower blood sugar, reduce phlegm and detoxify.

Lily Bulb Petals with Wolfberries and Red Dates 77

Mint Tea with Honey and Red Dates 77

Chrysanthemum Tea 79

Iron Goddess of Mercy Tea with Apple Slices 81

Lily Bulb Petals with Wolfberries and Red Dates

Cooking time: 45 minutes • Serves 4

Red dates are said to prevent skin problems, improve blood circulation and work against cell degeneration. They are also good for masking the less than pleasant flavours of strong-tasting herbs in a given blend. Do not discard the dates after cooking as they are rich in vitamins C and E.

Dried lily bulb petals
    (*bai he/bak hup*)
    60 g, rinsed
Dried red dates
    (*hong zao/hung cho*)
    15, pitted and rinsed
Chinese wolfberries
    (*gou qi zi/gei chi*)
    1 Tbsp, rinsed
Water 800 ml

1. Combine all ingredients in a pot. Bring to the boil. Simmer over low heat for 40 minutes. Serve warm or chilled.

Mint Tea with Honey and Red Dates
Cooking time: 20 minutes • Serves 4

Garden variety mint leaves are much underrated. Any herbalist will swear by their efficacy for a whole range of ills. Most immediately, mint helps to calm nerves, ease headaches and toothaches and reduce phlegm.

Water 600 ml
Fresh mint leaves
    30 g, washed and drained
Dried red dates
    (*hong zao/hung cho*)
    10, pitted
Honey 2 Tbsp

1. Bring water to the boil. Add mint leaves and dates. Simmer for 5 minutes. Turn off heat, cover and steep for 10 minutes.

2. Add honey. Stir to incorporate flavours. Discard mint leaves. Serve hot.

Opposite: Mint Tea with Honey and Red Dates.

Chrysanthemum Tea Cooking time: 30 minutes • Serves 4

No commercial product can ever surpass homemade chrysanthemum tea brewed from dried flowers obtainable from all herbal shops and some supermarkets. The best way to brew chrysanthemum tea is to steep the petals in freshly boiled water so infusion occurs over a prolonged period of time. Rapid boiling tends to dissipate the flavour. One of the best-known 'cooling' agents, chrysanthemum petals are also known for their detoxifying properties. Herbalists usually stock two types of chrysanthemum — yellow and white. The former reduces excess 'heat' in the body and treats flu symptoms, while the latter helps to soothe the lungs and reduce phlegm.

Water 2 litres
Rock sugar 150 g
Dried chrysanthemum petals 30 g

Time-saver
Although the result is arguably less flavourful, a faster way of making chrysanthemum tea is to combine all the ingredients in a pot and bring to the boil, simmer for 30 minutes, and then leave to cool. Strain and keep petals for a second round of weaker but still good chrysanthemum tea.

1. Bring water to the boil. Add rock sugar.

2. When sugar has completely dissolved, place dried chrysanthemum petals in an enamel or china teapot and pour sweetened water over. Cover and let seep for about 1 hour.

Iron Goddess of Mercy Tea with Apple Slices

Cooking time: 25 minutes • Serves 4

A type of black tea, Iron Goddess of Mercy (*tie guan yin/teet goon yam*), when brewed with apple slices, replenishes iron and improves metabolism. Iron Goddess of Mercy Tea is readily available in herbal shops and Chinese supermarkets. Alternatively, use any strong black tea. Tea leaves in general also contain essential amino acids and tannic acid that help aid digestion and lower blood pressure.

Iron Goddess of Mercy tea 1 Tbsp

Large apples (any variety) 2, peeled, cored and thinly sliced

Water 800 ml

1. Boil water. Infuse tea in a pot for 5 minutes.

2. Steep apple slices in tea for 15 minutes. Serve warm.

Savoury Stews

If there is one category of herbal cooking I enjoy dwelling at length upon, it is this one — the savoury herbal stew. Over centuries, recipes in this category have earned the reputation of being delicious, nourishing and extremely 'warming'. In order to appreciate them, one has to first understand the importance of liquid sustenance to the Chinese psyche. It is, to some extent, a throwback to rather more impoverished times when food was scarce and only the most watery gruel provided daily sustenance. Soups were created for their all-in-one ability to provide sustenance. Fuel, too, was scarce and cooking the family meal over one precious fire was a better option than flaring several clay ovens. Thus, soups have become an integral part of the Chinese meal, entirely different from their western counterpart. While the latter are meant to be appetisers, the former are borne with pride to the table to sit amid other dishes and be sipped ever so appreciatively through the meal. In fact, in days gone by, no Chinese meal would have been regarded as complete if it did not consist of "four plates and a bowl", alluding to four dishes, which may be stir-fried, braised or steamed, and the central bowl of hot, steaming soup.

Herbal soups rarely have a strong medicinal taste or bitterness characteristic of other medicinal herbs not usually used in daily cooking. It is also a fallacy that cooking these dishes is troublesome. Rather, the reverse is true once you have learnt the basic principles of herbal preparation: that the blend is all-important and that there are only three methods — slow cooking or simmering, steaming and double-boiling. Moreover, modern science has since contributed the pressure cooker, which should be viewed as a convenient and time-saving device rather than a culinary sell-out. All of the herbalists I have since spoken to dismissed the theory that pressure cooking is not acceptable because it diminishes nutritional value. Pressure cooking, in fact, traps in more nutrients by ensuring practically no evaporation. Tradition dies hard, nevertheless, and many elderly Chinese will still insist on simmering, maybe even over charcoal embers.

Chicken or Lean Pork with Ginseng Shreds 85

Chicken with Cordyceps and Chinese Yam 85

Chicken or Lean Pork with White Fungus 85

Chicken or Pork with Notoginseng Root 87

Lamb with Chinese Angelica and Astragalus Root 87

Pork with Eucommia Bark and Chinese Angelica 89

Pork with Falsestarwort and Lilyturf Roots, Apricot Kernels and Pears 89

Pork with Skullcap, Solomon's Seal, Lotus Seeds and Barley 91

Duck with Lotus Seeds, Barley and Tangerine Peel 91

Chicken with Korean Ginseng 93

Chicken with Ginseng and Foxglove Root 93

Black Chicken and Ginseng 94

Chicken with Bird's Nest and Ginseng 95

Chicken or Lean Pork with Bird's Nest 95

Chicken or Lean Pork with Solomon's Seal 96

Chicken or Lean Pork with Solomon's Seal and Chinese Yam 96

Chicken or Lean Pork and Ginseng's Top 97

Chicken or Lean Pork with Solomon's Seal, Chinese Yam and Wolfberries 97

Chicken and Chinese Angelica 98

Duck with Winter Melon, Gingko Nuts and Tangerine Peel 98

Pig's Heart with Lotus Seeds, Longan and Falsestarwort Root 99

Chicken Feet with Peanuts, Red Beans and Tangerine Peel 99

Chicken or Lean Pork with Ginseng Shreds

Cooking time: 1 hour • Serves 4

The ginseng called for in this recipe is not the root itself, but the thin, stringy roots that extend from the main stalk. The Cantonese call these shreds *yong sam soe*, which literally means the "beard of the ginseng root". The beard, as it were, is a mild form of the potent root and makes a good introduction for those who are consuming it for the first time. It is extremely palatable, with only a slight bitter taste and is good for restoring the body's 'heat'.

Chicken 1, about 1 kg, or
   600 g lean pork
Ginseng shreds 30 g
Water 1 litre
Salt 2 tsp

1. Clean chicken thoroughly. Remove head and feet, as well as skin if desired. If using pork, wash and leave in one piece.
2. Except salt, combine all other ingredients in a pot. Cover and bring to the boil. Simmer over low heat for about 1 hour. Add salt in the last few minutes of cooking.

Cooking Know-how

Although tradition often decrees that a whole bird is used, there is no reason why it cannot be substituted with chicken joints as there is no difference in flavour.

Chicken with Cordyceps and Chinese Yam

Cooking time: 1 hour 30 minutes • Serves 4

Chicken 1, about 900 g
Cordyceps (*dong chong
   xia cao/tung chung cho*)
   30 g, rinsed
Chinese yam (*shan yao/
   wai san*) 15 g, rinsed
Water 1.5 litres
Salt 2 tsp

1. Combine all ingredients in a pot. Simmer over very low heat for at least 1 hour 30 minutes. Before serving, skim off as much fat as possible.

Chicken or Lean Pork with White Fungus

Cooking time: 40 minutes • Serves 4

Chicken 1, about 1 kg, or
   400 g lean pork
White fungus (*bai mu er/
   shuet yi*) 30 g
Water 1 litre
Salt 2 tsp

1. Clean chicken thoroughly, and skin if desired. If using pork, trim off any fat if desired, but leave in one piece or cut into two large chunks.
2. Soak white fungus in warm water. Remove all impurities. Wash and drain slightly expanded fungus, squeezing out all moisture.
3. Except white fungus, combine all other ingredients in a pot. Simmer for 20 minutes. Add white fungus. Simmer for 20 minutes more.

Opposite: Chicken or Lean Pork with White Fungus.

Chicken or Pork with Notoginseng Root

Cooking time: 1 hour 30 minutes • Serves 4

Notoginseng is a pebble-like root with faint white specks and is believed to revitalise strained muscles and to right internal disorders. The root is usually prescribed to active people, especially those who participate in contact sports. In other words, the people most likely to suffer from strains, sprains and internal bruises.

Chicken 1, about 1 kg, or 600 g lean pork

Notoginseng root (*tian qi/ teen chat*) 30 g, rinsed and drained

Water 1 litre

Salt 2 tsp

1. Clean chicken thoroughly, and skin if desired. If using pork, trim off any fat and leave in one piece.

2. Combine all ingredients in a pot. Simmer for 1 hour 30 minutes.

Lamb with Chinese Angelica and Astragalus Root

Cooking time: 2 hours • Serves 4

This is a recipe from Dr. Geng's family treasure trove of restorative dishes, and one that I have tasted often. The recipe does take a little effort, with the lamb and herbs prepared separately. The recipe is recommended to those who need to improve Qi and to women after birth. Dr. Geng recently gave birth to a bonny baby girl and this has been her chief sustenance. She recommends using lamb on the bone.

Chinese angelica (*dang gui/dong kwai*) 5 g, rinsed

Astragalus root (*huang qi/ puk kei*) 20 g, rinsed

Dried red dates (*hong zao/hung cho*) 10, rinsed

Lamb on the bone 900 g, cut into chunks through the bone

Ginger 1 large knob, sliced

Water 1.5 litres, equally divided between two pots

Salt 2 tsp

1. Boil rinsed ingredients in one pot of water for 40 minutes.

2. Boil lamb pieces and ginger in second pot of water for about 1 hour. Alternatively, pressure cook for 30 minutes with slightly less liquid. The resulting lamb should fall away from the bone. When done, add salt.

3. The traditional way to serve this is to blend equal parts of the contents of each pot, lamb and stock with the herbal stock.

Opposite: Lamb with Chinese Angelica and Astragalus Root.

Pork with Eucommia Bark and Chinese Angelica

Cooking time: 1 hour • Serves 4

Eucommia bark reputedly detoxifies and is effective in the treatment of lumbago and muscular weakness. Chicken or mutton can be used in place of lean pork in this recipe.

Lean pork 750 g, washed, trimmed of excess fat and cut into large chunks

Eucommia bark (*du zhong/ dou chong*) 8 g, rinsed

Chinese angelica (*dang gui/dong kwai*) 8 g, rinsed

Dried red dates (*hong zao/ hung cho*) 10, pitted and rinsed

Salt 2 tsp

Carrot 1, cut into large chunks

1. Except carrot, combine all other ingredients in a pot. Bring to the boil. Simmer over lower heat for 45 minutes.

2. Add carrots. Simmer for 15 minutes more. Discard herbs, then serve hot.

Pork with Falsestarwort and Lilyturf Roots, Apricot Kernels and Pears
Cooking time: 1 hour • Serves 4

Both pears and lilyturf root are famous 'coolants' and this unusual blend is said to help alleviate dry coughs, moisten the lungs, balance *Qi* and promote *Yin* properties.

Lean pork 450 g

Falsestarwort root (*tai zi sheng/tai chi sam*) 15 g, washed and drained

Lilyturf root (*mai dong/ mak tung*) 15 g, washed and drained

Bitter apricot kernels (*bei xing/puk hung*) 20, washed and drained

Sweet apricot kernels (*nan xing/nam hung*) 20, washed and drained

Pears 4, peeled, cored and quartered

Salt 2 tsp

Water 1 litre

1. Combine all ingredients in a pot. Simmer for about 1 hour.

Cooking know-how

If you want to retain some of the bite in the pears, add them only in the last 30 minutes of cooking.

Opposite: Pork with Falsestarwort and Lilyturf Roots, Apricot Kernels and Pears.

Pork with Skullcap, Solomon's Seal, Lotus Seeds and Barley Cooking time: 2 hours • Serves 4

The full name of skullcap is barbat skullcap scutellaria, or ban zhi lian in Mandarin, and its botanical name is scutellaria barbata herba. Skullcap, when combined with the other herbs in this recipe, promotes good Qi and healthy spleen and stomach functions.

Dried lotus seeds 2 Tbsp
Barley 2 Tbsp
Skullcap 5 g, rinsed and drained
Solomon's seal (*yu zhu/ yok chok*) 10 g, rinsed and drained
Lean pork 450 g
Water 1 litre
Salt 2 tsp

1. Soak lotus seeds and barley for a few hours before cooking. Alternatively, separately boil them for 30 minutes. Precooked lotus seeds can be substituted to save some time.

2. Combine all ingredients in a pot. Cover and bring to the boil. Simmer over medium heat for 1–2 hours.

Duck with Lotus Seeds, Barley and Tangerine Peel
Cooking time: 2 hours • Serves 4

This may sound like an unlikely combination but the result is positively ambrosial if you like duck. This rich fowl is rarely given a chance to vindicate itself and most will simply turn up their noses on account of the duck's undeserved reputation for having a strong odour. Well-prepared duck has only the faintest odour and with the guilty glands removed from the region of the parson's nose, it can be the most beautiful bird. Remember, too, that duck is extremely fatty and unless you like a layer of duck fat floating on the surface of your soup, remove the skin.

Duck 1, about 1.5 kg
Barley 100 g, washed and drained
Dried tangerine peel 5 pieces
Water 2 litres
Salt 2 tsp
Ground white pepper (optional) 1 tsp
Precooked lotus seeds 40, washed and drained

1. Clean duck thoroughly. Cut off and discard head and feet, unless you have a passion for them. Cut remaining duck into 8 joints. Remove every shred of blood and entrails. Skin if desired Wash with plenty of salt. Drain well.

2. Except lotus seeds, combine all other ingredients in a pot. Cover and simmer for 2 hours. Check liquid level occasionally. Add lotus seeds in the last 20 minutes of simmering.

Time-saver
This recipe can be prepared with a pressure cooker. Halve the amount of water to 1 litre, simmer over medium heat for 45 minutes, then remove from heat. Add lotus seeds to cook, uncovered and without pressure. Simmer for 20 minutes. If soup is oily, allow to cool and remove layer of duck fat with a spoon.

Opposite: Duck with Lotus Seeds, Barley and Tangerine Peel.

Chicken with Korean Ginseng Cooking time: 1 hour • Serves 4

There are those who will gladly part with a great deal of money for a root of premium ginseng with the belief that it is a magical elixir. Korean ginseng (*gao li shen/go lai sam*) is quite similar to Chinese ginseng but is regarded by some as being more potent. At some food exhibitions where superior ginseng is kept under lock and key, Korean ginseng has been known to cost tens of thousands of dollars. This is not a soup to be sipped amid anything less than tranquil ambience. Like approaching the best wine, the state of mind brooks no distraction. Above all, the palate must be receptive to this herby nectar. If nothing else, you have spent a great deal of money for a few moments of pure culinary pleasure.

Chicken 1, about 900 g
Korean ginseng 60 g
Water 1 litre
Salt 2 tsp

1. Clean chicken thoroughly. Remove head, feet and/or skin as desired.

2. Combine all ingredients in a pot. Simmer for about 1 hour.

3. When you are satisfied with the taste and consistency of your precious soup, you absolutely must serve it in the finest porcelain.

Chicken with Ginseng and Foxglove Root Cooking time: 1 hour • Serves 4

Every now and then, herbalists will mention an uncertain category of ginseng (*pao shen/pao sam*) with no classifying name in English. While some herbalists define *pao shen* as American ginseng or a species of ginseng, others identify it more as a grade of ginseng, and a superior one at that. Where there is no confusion about *pao shen*, however, is its price. *Pao shen* is usually more expensive. Ask your herbalist to recommend what is best suited to this recipe. Foxglove root is prescribed by herbalists for the treatment of coughs, headaches, vertigo and low blood pressure, as well as for disorders of the kidney and lungs.

Chicken 1, about 1.5 kg
Ginseng (*pao shen/pau sam*) 20 g, rinsed and drained
Foxglove root (*shou di huang/sok tei*) 20 g, rinsed and drained
Water 1 litre
Salt 2 tsp

1. Combine all ingredients in a pot. Cover and simmer for 1 hour. Serve hot.

2. The resulting chicken meat would be relatively tasteless, but there is no sense in wasting it. Eat with a side dip of dark soy sauce.

Opposite: Chicken with Korean Ginseng.

Black Chicken and Ginseng Cooking time: 1 hour • Serves 4

Black chickens are generally smaller than their ordinary counterparts and have, for centuries, been deemed superior because of their said restorative properties. Colour and size aside, black chickens are no different in taste and texture. This recipe also does not require a specific type of ginseng and what you eventually put in the pot really depends on what you have selected at the shop.

Black chicken 1, about 650 g

Ginseng 15 g, rinsed and drained

Chinese angelica (*dang gui/dong kwai*) 30 g, rinsed and drained

Dried red dates (*hong zao/hung cho*) 10, pitted, rinsed and drained

Water 1 litre

Salt 2 tsp

1. Clean chicken thoroughly. Leave whole or cut into 4 large joints if preferred.

2. Combine all ingredients in a pot. Bring to the boil. Simmer over lower heat for 45 minutes or until chicken is tender.

3. Except dates, discard all herbs. Serve warm.

Chicken with Bird's Nest and Ginseng Cooking time: 1 hour • Serves 4

This is a herbier version of the previous recipe with the addition of ginseng. The tradition is also to use the best ginseng you can afford for economy has no place in the pursuit of good, nourishing Chinese soups.

Chicken 1, about 900 g
Bird's nest 100 g, soaked and thoroughly cleaned
Ginseng 60 g
Water 1 litre
Salt 2 tsp

1. Clean chicken thoroughly. Skin if desired.

2. Combine all ingredients in a pot. Simmer for at least 1 hour.

Cooking Know-how

The longer bird's nest is soaked prior to cooking, the softer it becomes. For this recipe, however, soaking the bird's nest for ages before cooking does not count for much because it is simmered for a prolonged period of time anyway.

Chicken or Lean Pork with Bird's Nest Cooking time: 1 hour • Serves 4

This is where bird's nest really shines — as a star ingredient in a savoury soup that is rich with all the natural goodness of chicken or lean pork. Perhaps more than any other combination, bird's nest and white meat in a lightly fragrant soup make not only warming sustenance, but also a classic palate refresher. It is for this reason that a light soup is sometimes served near the end of a multiple-course Chinese meal — to clean the palate after heavy dishes in preparation for what is yet to come.

Chicken 1, about 900 g, or 400 g lean pork
Bird's nest 90 g, soaked and thoroughly cleaned
Water 1 litre
Salt 2 tsp

1. Combine all ingredients in a pot. Simmer for 1 hour. Serve hot. Add a sprinkling of good, white pepper if desired.

2. If you are serving the family individual bowls of soup, it is as well to shred the chicken after removing all traces of skin and fat.

Chicken or Lean Pork with Solomon's Seal

Cooking time: 1 hour–1 hour 30 minutes • Serves 4

This is a clear soup made from either chicken or lean pork, depending on your preference. As chicken comes with a percentage of inedible bones and gristle, the amount specified is always more than that for pork. It is entirely optional whether the chicken is skinned or not, and likewise whether it is left whole or cut up. If using pork, it should be cut into large chunks, if at all, and not thin slices. While this is more a tradition than an instruction in pursuit of better nutritional results, a herbal soup somehow does not look right with thin slices of meat floating about.

Chicken 1, about 900 g, or 600 g lean pork

Solomon's seal (*yu zhu/ yok chok*) 15 g, rinsed and drained

Water 1 litre

Salt 2 tsp

1. Clean chicken thoroughly. Remove head and feet. If using pork, wash and leave in one piece.

2. Combine all ingredients in a pot. Simmer for between 1 hour and 1 hour 30 minutes, depending on heat intensity. Adjust to taste if necessary. Drink soup warm.

Chicken or Lean Pork with Solomon's Seal and Chinese Yam
Cooking time: 1 hour • Serves 4

When herbalists prescribe pork with a given blend, they will always recommend that you use the leanest cut possible. Pork fat may have little nutritional value, but the tiniest bit of fat renders any soup more flavourful and "smooth", as the Cantonese have come to describe with the term *wat*. Anything that is *wat* has a texture akin to that of butter-smoothness. In this recipe, however, the soup is drunk for nourishment and so the smoothness or *wat* factor is not as important.

Chicken 1, about 1 kg, or 600 g lean pork

Solomon's seal (*yu zhu/ yok chok*) 15 g, rinsed

Chinese yam (*shan yao/ wai san*) 15 g, rinsed

Water 1 litre

Salt 2 tsp

1. Clean chicken thoroughly. Remove excess fatty skin. Leave whole. If using pork, trim off any fat if desired, but leave in one piece.

2. Combine all ingredients in a pot. Simmer for about 1 hour.

Cooking Know-how

A certain amount of evaporation is expected with any slow simmering process, especially if the pot used does not have a snug-fitting lid. Evaporation, however, also means a reduction of liquid and consequently a concentration of flavour. Expect about 20 per cent of reduction for every hour of simmering, although a lot depends on heat intensity and size of pot. As long as the final yield is about 4 medium-sized bowls, each about 500 ml, the proportion of water is correct.

Chicken or Lean Pork and Ginseng's Top

Cooking time: 45 minutes • Serves 4

The ginseng called for in this recipe is neither the main stalk nor the shreds, but the top and thicker end of the main stalk called *yong sam tau* by the Cantonese and means the "head of the ginseng root". The 'head' of the ginseng is stronger in flavour than the 'beard' and is also said to possess more Yang energy. Although this recipe says to use either chicken or pork, a combination of half and half is also plausible.

Spring chicken 1, about 400 g, or 400 g lean pork

Ginseng's top 30 g

Water 1 litre

Salt 2 tsp

1. Clean chicken thoroughly. Remove head and feet. It is unnecessary to skin a spring chicken as it is already lean. If using pork, wash and leave in one piece.

2. Combine all ingredients in a pot. Simmer for 45 minutes.

Cooking Know-how

A spring chicken does not need much more than 45 minutes of simmering to have most of its flavour and goodness extracted. It is useful to remember here that the true test of herbal soups lies not in how tender the meat is but how flavourful the soup has become.

Chicken or Lean Pork with Solomon's Seal, Chinese Yam and Wolfberries
Cooking time: 1 hour • Serves 4

Chinese wolfberries are reputedly good for the eyes and have a delicately sweet flavour. Children are often given a few of them to munch straight off the medicinal shop counter, but they are best simmered with poultry or robust meats like lamb or mutton. As a rough guide, use a handful or about 2 Tbsp for every 4 serves of soup.

Chicken 1, about 900 g, or 600 g lean pork

Solomon's seal (*yu zhu/ yok chok*) 15 g, rinsed

Chinese yam (*shan yao/ wai san*) 15 g, rinsed

Chinese wolfberries (*gou qi zi/gei chi*) 2 Tbsp, rinsed

Water 1.5 litres

Salt 2 tsp

1. Clean chicken thoroughly. Remove excess fatty skin. Either leave whole or cut into large joints. If using pork, cut into bite-sized chunks.

2. Combine all ingredients in a pot. Simmer for about 1 hour.

3. Garnish with a sprinkling of ground white pepper and fresh coriander (cilantro) leaves, also known as Chinese parsley.

Cooking Know-how

If you are making this dish in advance, allow to cool completely before skimming off fat from the surface for a less oily dish. If guests are involved, try serving the soup in shim bowls with lids for what seems to me to be the epitome of civilised dining.

Chicken and Chinese Angelica Cooking time: 1 hour • Serves 4

Chinese angelica is usually prescribed for gynaecological disorders but there is absolutely no reason why non-sufferers cannot enjoy it. For new mothers with a bout of those post-natal blues, try nursing them with some of this chicken soup. Discard not a single shred of chicken except gristle and bone, and down the soup to the last drop.

Chicken 1, about 1.5 kg

Chinese angelica
   (*dang gui/dong kwai*)
   30 g, rinsed

Water 1.5 litres

Salt 2 tsp

1. Clean chicken thoroughly. Leave skin on and whole.

2. Combine all ingredients in a pot. Simmer for about 1 hour.

Duck with Winter Melon, Gingko Nuts and Tangerine Peel Cooking time: 1 hour 30 minutes • Serves 4

The combined balance of a strong-flavoured meat like duck, delicate winter melon, a hint of tangerine and the mildly bitter gingko nuts is particularly captivating.

Duck 1, about 2 kg

Winter melon 1, about
   450 g

Dried tangerine peel
   4–5 pieces

Water 2 litres

Salt 2 tsp

Precooked gingko nuts
   40, washed and drained

1. Clean duck thoroughly. Remove head and feet. Cut into 8 large joints.

2. Peel winter melon, then halve. Remove soft centre and seeds. Cut remaining flesh into large chunks. Wash and drain.

3. Except gingko nuts and winter melon, combine all other ingredients in a pot. Simmer for about 1 hour. Add remaining ingredients. Simmer for 30 minutes more.

Time-saver

If using a pressure cooker, halve the specified amount of water to 1 litre. Except winter melon chunks and precooked gingko nuts, combine all other ingredients and pressure cook for 30 minutes. Add remaining ingredients. Pressure cook for 15 minutes more. If using dried gingko nuts, they should be soaked for several hours and then added for the entire pressure cooking time.

Pig's Heart with Lotus Seeds, Longan and Falsestarwort Root
Cooking time: 1 hour • Serves 4

Whatever your feelings about the animal's organ, this recipe helps calm nerves and reduces palpitations and insomnia.

Pig's heart 1, about 300 g
Dried lotus seeds 20 g
Falsestarwort root
  (*tai zi sheng/tai chi sam*)
  10 g, washed and drained
Dried longan flesh
  10 g, washed and drained
Water 1 litre
Salt 2 tsp

1. Wash pig's heart. Trim off tendons and remove traces of blood. Leave whole or cut into two large pieces.

2. Boil lotus seeds for 30 minutes. Drain. Alternatively, precooked lotus seeds can be substituted to save some time.

3. Combine all ingredients in a pot. Simmer for 1 hour.

Chicken Feet with Peanuts, Red Beans and Tangerine Peel
Cooking time: 2-3 hours • Serves 4

Those unaccustomed might assume chicken feet here refer to the meaty thighs or legs. They do not. Chicken feet in this recipe are the scaly, bony lower limbs, claws included. They also happen to be delicious if treated right. It is no more uncivilized eating them than salivating over blue cheese. Never mind that chicken feet are extraordinarily cheap and usually ignored, they can still be coaxed to part with substantial nutrition and flavour. Besides, there is as much nutrition in the peanuts and red beans as there is flavour in the dried tangerine peel. Some Chinese believe that children given a steady diet of this dish will develop strong muscles.

Chicken feet 20–30
Shelled raw peanuts 150 g
Red (adzuki) beans 100 g,
  washed and drained
Dried tangerine peel
  4–5 pieces
Water 2 litres
Salt 3 tsp

1. Remove scaly outer skin of chicken feet. Cut off sharp talons. Wash in several changes of water. Drain.

2. Boil peanuts for a few minutes. Allow to cool before rubbing off skins if necessary.

3. Combine all ingredients in a pot. Simmer for 2–3 hours.

Cooking Know-how

If you are disinclined to prepare so many ingredients, simply combine chicken feet and peanuts in a pressure cooker for about 1 hour for a quick-and-easy soup.

Double-boiled Dishes

Although this is not a method of cooking that endears itself to anyone living in the fast lane of life, it is one that has transcended all social and economic barriers through centuries of Chinese culinary history. Although some may regard the whole business of cooking as a tedious chore if it deviates even slightly from microwave heating, it is really their loss for not finding the true joy of good food cooked with tender loving care.

Double-boiling is a technique that involves placing food in a container that sits suspended inside another, larger container. The latter of which contains a modest amount of boiling water and is what sits over the flame or source of heat. As such, the food has no direct contact with heat, and steam from the boiling water is all that powers the gentle simmering characteristic of double-boiled cooking. Food in a double-boiler does not so much boil as bubble and shudder over a long period of time. There is also no chance of burning and evaporation is minimal, so most nutrients are really sealed in provided the smaller container has a snug-fitting lid. Unlike the relatively makeshift bain-marie, the French method of cooking over boiling water European cooks employ for delicate custards and junkets to prevent burning and curdling, little steam escapes from the sides of a double-boiler.

There are several fundamental rules in double-boiling. First, water in the larger container should never be at a level that will force the smaller container upward like a driven piston when it boils; this simply means that too much water was added. Second, always have on standby boiling or at least hot water to add to the larger, outer container when needed so the cooking temperature does not drop suddenly as it would if you had added cold water. Third, double-boilers should only be placed over low to medium heat.

Just about every stew, soup, gruel or liquid-based dish may be double-boiled with pleasing results. It is particularly good for food that tends to break up with prolonged simmering.

Pork with Figs and Falsestarwort Root Cooking time: 1 hour • Serves 4

This double-boiled dish from Dr. Geng helps to promote *Qi*, strengthens the immunity system and blood function and improves the digestive process.

Lean pork 250 g, sliced into thick pieces

Fresh figs 4, stems removed and left whole

Falsestarwort root (*tai zi shen/tai chi sam*) 20 g, washed and drained

Salt 2 tsp

Water 750 ml

1. Combine all ingredients in a double-boiler. Simmer for 1 hour or until pork is very tender.

Cooking know-how

Dried figs, if available, can also be used for this dish. Note, however, that some vendors sell them sugared.

Bird's Nest and Chicken Cooking time: 2 hours • Serves 4

Of all the double-boiled dishes, this one is perhaps the most frequently cooked. With only bird's nest and chicken as ingredients, there is not the slightest hint of herbal flavour, appeasing people who might find even the mildest herb off-putting. It is basically a light, refreshing soup that can be drunk at any time of the day.

Chicken 1, about 900 g

Bird's nest 60 g, washed and thoroughly cleaned

Water 1 litre

Salt 2 tsp

1. Clean chicken thoroughly. Remove head and feet, as well as skin if desired.

2. Combine all ingredients in a double-boiler. Simmer for 2 hours.

Cooking Know-how

It does not make one jot of difference to the nourishment of the dish if you do include gizzard in this recipe. The presence of gizzard only darkens the soup.

Opposite: Pork with Figs and Falsestarwort Root.

Duck with Longan, Cordyceps, Chinese Yam and Wolfberries Cooking time: 1 hour • Serves 4

This soup is inclined to be fatty even after skinning the duck, so if you prefer a clearer soup, use chicken instead. The addition of longan renders the soup rather sweet, so adjust the amount used according to taste.

Duck 1, about 1.5 kg

Dried longan flesh
100 g, washed and
thoroughly cleaned

Cordyceps (*tung chung
xia cao/tung chong cho*)
20 g

Chinese yam (*shan yao/
wai san*) 15 g

Chinese wolfberries
(*gou qi zi/gei chi*) 2 Tbsp

Water 1.5 litres

Salt 2 tsp

1. Wash and clean duck thoroughly. Remove head, feet and skin, as well as any traces of blood.

2. Combine all ingredients in a double-boiler. Simmer for 3 hours. Add boiling water to outer pot if necessary. Evaporation from the inner pot is generally minimal, but check after 2 hours and add boiling or hot water if necessary.

Cooking Know-how

If you wish to substitute duck with chicken in this recipe, the chicken used should be about 1 kg. Correspondingly, water should be reduced to 1 litre and cooking time to 1 hour 30 minutes.

Mutton and Chinese Angelica Cooking time: 2-3 hours • Serves 4

Although Chinese angelica is typically recommended for women with after-birth problems, it is perfectly palatable and nourishing for everyone in the family. The herb has a strong flavour that combines well with hearty meats like mutton but is equally tasty with chicken. The strength of this soup depends on the type of Chinese angelica used.

Chinese angelica
(*dang gui/dong kwai*)
30 g, sliced

Mutton 450 g, washed and
cut into large chunks

Water 1 litre

Salt 2 tsp

1. Combine all ingredients in a double-boiler. Simmer for 2–3 hours.

Cooking Know-how

For all double-boiled soups or stews, add just enough liquid to cover ingredients for full flavour.

Frog's Legs with Gingko Nuts and Chinese Wolfberries
Cooking time: 2 hours • Serves 4

There is no need to agonise about where and how to acquire frog's legs as many supermarkets and even some wet markets sell them all nicely skinned and cleaned. Frog's legs are never sold with the carcass, only as lower limbs. For those unfamiliar with this delicacy, frog's legs taste like chicken but are in fact, more tender. They are not at all expensive and the little thighs have a surprising amount of meat on them. You will find this soup reminiscent of chicken broth.

Frog's legs 450 g, washed and left whole
Chinese wolfberries (*gou qi zi/gei chi*) 2 Tbsp
Precooked gingko nuts 40
Water 1 litre
Salt 2 tsp
Ground black pepper ½ tsp

1. Combine all ingredients in a double-boiler. Simmer for 2 hours.

Pigeon and Bird's Nest
Cooking time: 2 hours • Serves 4

This is a light and delicious soup that, despite the lack of herbs, is still nourishing for the bird's nest. Often served midway through Chinese banquets to refresh the palate, this is a fairly costly dish, but there is also a more inexpensive improvisation — substitute bird's nest with white fungus that is often termed mock bird's nest.

Pigeons 2, total weight 600 g
Bird's nest 60 g, soaked and thoroughly cleaned
Salt 2 tsp
Water 1 litre
Sesame oil 1 tsp
Ground white pepper 1 pinch

1. Clean pigeons thoroughly. Remove heads and legs.
2. Except sesame oil and pepper, combine all other ingredients in a double-boiler. Simmer over low heat for 2 hours. Add sesame oil and pepper before serving.

Cooking Know-how
If pigeon is unavailable, quail can be used as a substitute.

Chicken with Cordyceps, Chinese Yam and Wolfberries

Cooking time: 2-3 hours • Serves 4

This is a particularly nourishing soup that, despite the multiple-herb mix, does not taste at all strange. Both Chinese yam and wolfberries have mild flavours, and the cordyceps impart to the soup a slight bitterness that is also palatable. The predominant flavour remains that from the chicken.

Chicken 1, about 900 g

Cordyceps (*dong chong xia cao/tung chung cho*) 30 g

Chinese yam (*shan yao/ wai san*) 15 g

Chinese wolfberries (*gou qi zi/gei chi*) 2 Tbsp

Water 1 litre

Salt 2 tsp

1. Clean chicken thoroughly. Remove excess fatty skin. Leave whole or cut into 4 large joints.

2. Combine all ingredients in a double-boiler. Simmer over medium heat for 2–3 hours. There is rarely a need to add liquid to the inner pot, but top up with hot water if necessary.

Cooking Know-how

When cooking with a double-boiler, water in the larger container should never boil over. If it does, it means that the container was over-filled.

Chicken and Ginseng Cooking time: 1 hour • Serves 4

Because of the ginseng, the cost of this soup lies anywhere between a few dollars and a king's ransom. While the belief is that the more you pay, the better the nourishment you get, the theory does not necessarily apply to taste.

Chicken 1, about 900 g

Ginseng 30 g

Water 1 litre

Salt 2 tsp

1. Clean chicken thoroughly. Remove head, neck and feet, as well as skin if desired.

2. Combine all ingredients in a double-boiler. Simmer for 1 hour.

Cooking Know-how

Variations of this recipe can be created by substituting chicken with duck or lean pork. While the rest of the ingredients remain unchanged in quantity, the cooking times vary somewhat. Duck needs to be double-boiled for 2 hours and pork for 1 hour 30 minutes. It is also common practice to combine chicken and pork.

Chicken Feet and Pig's Brain with Astragalus Root, Chinese Yam and Wolfberries Cooking time: 1 hour 30 minutes • Serves 4

This compote of ingredients is wondrously aromatic and absolutely delicious. Pale cream in colour, astragalus root is good for improving blood circulation. While pig's brain may not be everyone's cup of tea, it is very much an accepted part of herbal cooking. There must be at least a dozen ways to cook pig's brain but gentle simmering is by far the best as it is an extremely delicate variety of meat.

Chicken feet 20, washed, stripped of scaly skin and talons removed

Pig's brain 1, thoroughly cleaned

Astragalus root (*huang qi/ puk kei*) 5 pieces

Chinese yam (*shan yao/ wai san*) 15 g

Chinese wolfberries (*gou qi zi/gei chi*) 2 Tbsp

Water 1 litre

Salt 2 tsp

Grated fresh ginger (**optional**) 1 Tbsp

1. Except ginger, combine all other ingredients in a double-boiler. Make sure brain is not squashed. Simmer for 1 hour 30 minutes. Serve with ginger if desired.

Cooking know-how

To clean pig's brain, first soak it in a bowl of water, then drain off any blood until water is clear. To get pig's brain really clean, use a pointed toothpick to pick up one end of a capillary, a tiny blood vessel, and roll it off gently. Each brain has many criss-crossing capillaries. Repeat until brain is completely free of them.

Chicken, Bird's Nest and Ginseng Cooking time: 2 hours • Serves 4

This is an all-time favourite of mine even if it does cost a pretty penny. On lean days, I buy loose pieces of bird's nest for a few dollars, use a mere hint of ginseng and splurge on the chicken. After all, how much can a chicken cost? Nevertheless, it is the chicken that I tear into after consuming the soup even though it is relatively tasteless. My mother used to make a decent dish of the double-boiled chicken. She would cut the drained chicken into large joints, and then deep-fry them after marinating them in dark soy sauce.

Chicken 1, about 900 g

Bird's nest 60 g, washed and thoroughly cleaned

Ginseng 15 g

Water 1 litre

Salt 2 tsp

1. Skin and clean chicken thoroughly. When bird's nest is also part of the recipe, the chicken used should be as lean as possible because the resulting soup should be clear and light for the flavour of the bird's nest to come through.

2. Combine all ingredients in a double-boiler. Simmer for 2 hours.

Duck with Cordyceps, Foxglove Root and Red Dates

Cooking time: 2 hours • Serves 6

Cordyceps and foxglove root together help to strengthen kidney function and the lungs. The mighty combination is also said to alleviate coughs and night sweats.

Duck 1, cleaned and trimmed

Cordyceps (*dong chong xia cao/tung chung cho*) 5 g, washed and drained

Dried red dates (*hong zao/hung cho*) 10, washed and drained

Foxglove root (*shou di huang/sok dei*) 15 g

Salt 2 tsp

Water 1 litre

1. Combine all ingredients in a double-boiler. Simmer for at least 2 hours or until duck is fork tender.

Cooking Know-how

If you can find French-cut duck breasts, substitute whole duck with 700 g duck breast for a much less oily dish. Skinned, the duck breasts consist of mostly lean meat.

White Fungus and Chicken Cooking time: 1 hour 30 minutes • Serves 4

For want of a better description, this dish is a watered-down version of bird's nest and chicken. Nevertheless, it is a delicious soup with crunch from the white fungus that bird's nest does not have.

Chicken 1, about 900 g

White fungus (*bai mu er/ shuet yi*) 100 g, soaked and thoroughly cleaned

Water 1 litre

Salt 2 tsp

Light soy sauce 1 tsp

Ground white pepper 1 tsp

Fresh coriander leaves (cilantro)

1. Clean chicken thoroughly. Remove head and feet if desired, but do not skin. This soup is tastier with a little fat in it.

2. Combine chicken, white fungus, water and salt in a double- boiler. Simmer for 1 hour 30 minutes. Serve hot with light soy sauce, pepper and coriander.

Cooking Know-how

Pieces of white fungus are pale yellow and each have a hard bit attached. Snip this off before soaking. Also, if after soaking you find that you have a little more than you need, keep the excess in a covered container for use another day.

Notoginseng Root and Chicken Cooking time: 2 hours • Serves 4

Notoginseng root looks like a stone and rather unappealing at first sight, but it has been brewed for centuries for specific ailments like internal bruising and, if you would so believe, a diminished male libido! My first personal experience with notoginseng occurred some years ago after a small army-training accident. I had fallen into a U-boat and bashed myself in a few places that rendered me so sore that I was somewhat immobile for a month. When I came home from hospital, I was advised to drink this brew for a week. I certainly recovered.

Chicken 1, about 900 g

Notoginseng root (*tian qi/ teen chat*) 30 g

Water 1 litre

Salt 2 tsp

Light soy sauce 1 tsp

Ground white pepper 1 tsp

1. Except light soy sauce and pepper, combine all other ingredients in a double-boiler. Simmer for 2 hours.

2. The addition of soy sauce before serving is a personal habit as I rather prefer the rich saltiness of this ingredient to plain salt. Also, pepper gives any savoury soup a kick and helps it go down, especially when you are not particularly fond of strong herbs.

Spare Ribs with Chinese Yam, Angelica and Wolfberries

Cooking time: 2 hours • Serves 2

Chinese yam aids the lungs and kidneys and generally nourishes the whole body. All cuts of pork, including spare ribs, are deemed 'neutral' and could become Yin or Yang in energy, depending on the herbs used. This is a 'warming' or Yang dish and is especially good for women after giving birth.

Pork spare ribs 500 g, cut into large pieces and excess fat trimmed

Chinese yam (*shan yao/ wai san*) 8 g, rinsed and drained

Chinese angelica (*dang gui/dong kwai*) 8 g, rinsed and drained

Chinese wolfberries (*gou qi zi/gei chi*) 2 Tbsp, rinsed and drained

Water 1 litre

Salt 2 tsp

1. Combine all ingredients in a double-boiler. Cook over medium heat for 2 hours. Discard herbs. Serve with rice.

Cooking Know-how

This recipe can also be prepared through conventional stove-top cooking, gas or electric. In a covered pot, simmer over medium heat for about 1 hour.

Herbal One-pot Meals

This category encompasses a range of dishes cooked frequently at home and in some restaurants. Most of these dishes are rich and complex experiences, and a number are also expensive to prepare by virtue of the cost of such ingredients as dried scallops, abalone and quality Chinese mushrooms.

Cooking these dishes at home should present little trouble once you understand the principles of slow cooking, the characteristics of each ingredient and the concepts of balancing and blending flavours. There is also much less mystique in these dishes as they are eaten more for their taste than their curative properties. Within the range of recipes lie many possibilities to create new and interesting dishes as guided by your preferences in taste and texture. For instance, lotus root is known to go well with pork spare ribs, but you may well wish to try combining it with chestnuts and pig's tripe instead. Unorthodox perhaps, but not to say it cannot be nutritious and tasty.

The most arresting feature of these dishes is that the amounts of ingredients specified are not derived from an exacting science. Whether you use 20 chestnuts with one chicken or 40 chestnuts with half a chicken makes little difference to the ultimate enjoyment of the dish. It is only a question of striking a perfect balance of flavours and textures for youself, finding the personal formula that pleases. These are also the dishes you can cook and present with great pride and flourish when you want to entertain special guests. They are elegant and say alot about a cook's flair for delicate composition.

Stuffed Pigeon with Chestnuts
and Lotus Seeds 115

Abalone with Ginseng and Peppercorns 115

Bean Curd Sticks and Gingko Nuts
with Pig's Tripe 117

Mutton with Longan, Chinese Yam and
Wolfberries 117

Eucommia Bark with Chicken and Pork 119

Chicken and Mushrooms with Chinese
Angelica and Astragalus Root in Wine 119

Dried Cuttlefish and Pork Ribs
with Lotus Root Soup 121

Pig's Tripe with Peppercorns 121

Duck and Dried Oysters with Chinese
Wolfberries and Lotus Seeds 123

Bean Curd Sticks and Gingko Nuts
with Eggs 123

Mutton Soup with Barley, Chinese Angelica
and Wolfberries 125

Euryale Seeds and Longan 125

Oxtail with Carrots and Eucommia Bark 127

Double-cooked Pork with Apricot Kernels
and Lotus Seeds 127

Chicken with Mushrooms and
Chinese Wolfberries 129

Braised Belly Pork with Chestnuts and
Chinese Wolfberries 129

Dried Scallops, Brown Marrow
and Pork Ribs 131

Chicken Stuffed with
Codonopsis Root 131

Dried Scallops and Pig's Tripe
with Chinese Wolfberries 133

Duck with Chinese Honeyed Dates
and Tangerine Peel 133

Mushroom with Chestnuts
and Lily Bulb Petals 135

Duck with Chinese Angelica
and Wine 135

Steamed Winter Melon with Crabmeat,
Chestnuts, Lotus Seeds and Barley 137

Chicken with Ginseng
and Lotus Root Soup 137

Chicken Broth with Barley, Euryale
and Lotus Seeds 139

Chicken with Gingko Nuts, Lotus Seeds
and Chinese Wolfberries 139

Mixed Meat Hotpot with Lotus Seeds
and Chrysanthemum 141

Beef and Yam with Ginseng, Chinese Yam
and Wolfberries 141

Fish with Cordyceps and
Chinese Wolfberries 143

Abalone and Chicken with Chinese Yam 143

Buddha's Feast 145

Chicken with Chestnuts and
Chinese Wolfberries 147

Dried Scallops, Lotus Seeds and Chinese
Angelica in Winter Melon 147

Stuffed Pigeon with Chestnuts and Lotus Seeds
Cooking time: 45 minutes • Serves 4

Dismiss the notion that a fat, cooing pigeon is an adorable living creature and you will be able to eat this dish without the slightest bit of queasiness. Deep-fried pigeons have been a banquet delicacy for as long as I can remember, and provided I do not have to kill the birds myself, I would eat them with gusto. Do not believe the old wives' tale that the only way to kill pigeons is by suffocating them. Instead, buy prepared pigeons from supermarkets. Humane sentiments aside, pigeon meat is sweeter and more tender than chicken.

Pigeons 2, total weight about 600 g

Dried chestnuts 40, boiled for 15 minutes and with skins rubbed off when cooled, then washed and drained

Precooked lotus seeds 40, washed and drained

Salt 2 tsp

Ground black pepper 1/2 tsp

Water 1 litre

1. Clean pigeons thoroughly. Remove heads and feet. Wash and drain.

2. Except water, combine all other ingredients. Stuff mixture into pigeons.

3. Place pigeons in a deep pot. Add enough water to just cover birds. Simmer for 45 minutes. Serve hot.

Abalone with Ginseng and Peppercorns
Cooking time: 1 hour • Serves 4

This princely concoction will make you weep with pleasure if you do it right, and without the slightest regard for economy. Canned abalone is generally expensive, but even more costly is its dried counterparts, which many Chinese medicinal shops sell. The greatest downside of dried abalone, however, is the lengthy and fiddly processing required before cooking. While the price of ginseng has the sky for its limit, there is always the option of using lower grade ginseng that will not break the bank.

Canned abalone 450 g, drained and thinly sliced

Ginseng 30 g

White peppercorns 1 Tbsp

Water 750 ml

Salt 2 tsp

1. Combine all ingredients in a small casserole. Make sure abalone slices are submerged. Cover and simmer for about 1 hour or until abalone is tender.

2. If you wish to thicken the gravy a little, add 1 tsp corn flour (cornstarch) dissolved in water at the end of cooking time.

Opposite: Abalone with Ginseng and Peppercorns.

Bean Curd Sticks and Gingko Nuts with Pig's Tripe

Cooking time: 1 hour 30 minutes • Serves 4

Bean curd sticks (*fu zhu/ fu chok*) 150 g, soaked until soft

Precooked gingko nuts 40

Precooked pig's tripe 200 g, cut into bite-sized pieces

Water 2 litres

Salt 2 tsp

Ground white pepper 1 tsp

1. Cut soft bean curd sticks into 5-cm pieces. Wash and drain.

2. If precooked gingko nuts are unavailable, soak dried ones in water until soft. Remove skins and bitter cores if necessary.

3. If precooked tripe is unavailable, refer to recipe *Pig's Tripe with Peppercorns* (pg 121) for how to prepare unprocessed tripe at home.

4. Combine all ingredients in a pot. Simmer for 1 hour 30 minutes. Serve hot.

Mutton with Longan, Chinese Yam and Wolfberries

Cooking time: 2 hours • Serves 4

This is a very rich soup that takes on the character of a stew if you reduce the amount of liquid used. Believers of Yin-Yang in food will defend the heartiness and 'warming' properties of mutton on a cold day. Lamb can be used as a substitute, but you will not get the characteristically rich flavour that only mutton gives. Chinese yam is used to promote vigour, and longan gives the soup a fragrant sweetness while counteracting some of the mutton fat.

Lean mutton 450 g, cut into large chunks and excess fat and gristle trimmed

Dried longan flesh 30 g, washed and thoroughly cleaned

Chinese yam (*shan yao/ wai san*) 10 slivers

Chinese wolfberries (*gou qi zi/gei chi*) 2 Tbsp

Water 1.5 litres

Salt 2 tsp

1. Combine all ingredients in a pot. Simmer for 2 hours. Skim off any fat floating on top. Serve hot. This dish is especially nice when served in a clay pot.

Cooking Know-how

In western countries, where goats are not generally farmed, the meat of older sheep is called mutton. It is not as gamy as goat but is just as good in flavour.

Opposite: Mutton with Longan, Chinese Yam and Wolfberries.

Eucommia Bark with Chicken and Pork Cooking time: 1 hour • Serves 4

Eucommia bark is identifiable by the silvery-white, floss-like shreds that are exposed in the crevices of its dried, cracked surface. Those very shreds are reputed to be good for aiding recovery from back and spinal ailments. It is one of the most popular herbs among herbal chefs.

Chicken 1, about 700 g

Lean pork 300 g, cut into large chunks and excess fat trimmed

Eucommia bark (*du zhong/dou chong*) 20 g

Water 1 litre

Salt 2 tsp

1. Clean chicken. Remove all evidence of marrow and blood. Cut into large joints.

2. Combine all ingredients in a pot. Simmer for 1 hour. Serve as a savoury soup with a meal.

Chicken and Mushrooms with Chinese Angelica and Astragalus Root in Wine Cooking time: 1 hour • Serves 4

A masterly blend of chicken, herbs, mushrooms and wine, this makes for an extremely 'warming' dish, particularly for new mothers because the Chinese angelica and astragalus root help to replenish the vital essences of the liver and heart. Although there is quite a lot of wine, most of the alcohol evaporates after boiling and can be drunk by even the strictest teetotaler.

Chicken 1, about 900 g

Dried Chinese mushrooms 8

Chinese angelica (*dang gui/dong kwai*) 30 g, rinsed

Astragalus root (*huang qi/ puk kei*) 30 g, rinsed

Chinese cooking wine (*hua diao/fa dew*) 500 ml

Water 500 ml

Salt 2 tsp

1. Clean chicken thoroughly. Cut into 8 joints. Remove excess fatty skin or skin entirely if you prefer a clear soup.

2. Soak mushrooms in hot water until very soft. Trim off hard stalks. Keep whole or slice each into two if very large.

3. Place rinsed herbs at the bottom of a pot. Add all other ingredients. Simmer over low heat for 1 hour. Adjust to taste with more salt if needed.

Cooking Know-how

If you souse the chicken in half the amount of wine allowed, the resulting cooked chicken will be much more flavourful.

Opposite: Chicken and Mushrooms with Chinese Angelica and Astragalus Root in Wine.

Dried Cuttlefish and Pork Ribs with Lotus Root Soup

Cooking time: 1 hour • Serves 4

Stewed long and lovingly, this soup has a near-perfect combination of flavours. Do not be put off by the coating of mud you see on lotus roots sold at wet markets. This actually means that they are fresh as can be, and they only need to be washed and scraped of the brown skin before cooking.

Cleaned lotus root 400 g, diagonally cut into 1-cm thick slices and soaked in cold water

Dried cuttlefish 15 g, washed

Pork ribs 400 g, washed and excess fat trimmed

Water 1.5 litres

Salt 1 tsp

Light soy sauce 1 Tbsp

1. Use kitchen scissors to cut cuttlefish into 1-cm wide pieces. Remove each hard bit that connects the tentacles and body. Snip tentacles into similarly sized pieces.

2. Combine all ingredients in a pot. Simmer for 1 hour. Adjust to taste with seasoning. Serve hot.

Cooking Know-how

If you are using dried lotus root slices, soak them for at least several hours or overnight before cooking.

Pig's Tripe with Peppercorns
Cooking time: 3-4 hours • Serves 4

Served on the premise of restoring post-natal weakness, this rich stew has been coaxed down the throats of many new mothers. The infusion of lots of peppercorns helps to restore the body's 'heat' and *Qi* believed to be lost in the process of child-bearing.

Precooked pig's tripe 300 g

White peppercorns 250 g, washed

Water 2 litres

Salt 2 tsp

1. Place peppercorns in stomach cavity. Sew up with thread to secure.

2. Combine all ingredients in a pot. Stew over low heat for 3–4 hours.

Cooking Know-how

If precooked tripe is unavailable, buy 1 set of pig's tripe from the butcher and clean it yourself at home. Wash pieces inside and out with plenty of salt until they are no longer slimy to the touch. Drain. Heat a dry wok until smoking, then singe tripe pieces thoroughly. An optional step, add 1 tsp bicarbonate of soda to lightly bleach pieces. When done, with pieces partially cooked, remove from wok, wash again and drain.

This recipe can also be double-boiled, which takes about 3 hours, or pressure cooked, which takes about 1 hour 30 minutes. Halve the specified amount of water to 1 litre for either method.

Opposite: Dried Cuttlefish and Pork Ribs with Lotus Root Soup.

Duck and Dried Oysters with Chinese Wolfberries and Lotus Seeds
Cooking time: 2 hours 30 minutes • Serves 4

This is a magnificent dish for the flavours it encapsulates. Be warned, however, that you will end up with at least 300 ml of duck fat, although it can be skimmed off easily, especially if you refrigerate to allow coagulation. The dish, in fact, tastes better the next day, after it has been clarified.

Duck 1 whole, about 2 kg
Dark soy sauce 2 Tbsp
Cooking oil 3 Tbsp
Dried oysters 15, soaked in hot water and drained
Precooked lotus seeds 30
Chinese wolfberries (*gou qi zi/gei chi*) 2 Tbsp
Chinese cooking wine (*hua diao/fa diew*) (optional) 2 Tbsp
Oyster sauce 2 Tbsp
Sugar 1 tsp
Salt 2 tsp
Water 2 litres

1. Clean duck thoroughly. Pat dry with kitchen paper. Remove only webbed feet. If you are confident of the task — believe me, it requires the utmost skill to do it — debone the whole duck so it resembles a deflated balloon. Rub all over with dark soy sauce. Allow to dry.

2. Heat half the oil in a non-stick wok. Singe duck all over until skin is brown and taut. Set aside. This step is not compulsory, but it does make the dish look more appetising by leading to a rich brown colour; it is otherwise pale beige.

3. Heat remaining oil. Add dried oysters, lotus seeds and wolfberries. Fry for 1–2 minutes. Add wine, oyster sauce, sugar, salt, and just enough water to bind the mixture to a suitable thickness for stuffing.

4. Allow mixture to cool slightly, then stuff into duck. Sew up with thread to seal cavity. Place in a deep casserole. Spread excess stuffing around duck. Add water. If liquid seems a bit pale, add 1 Tbsp dark soy sauce mixed with 1 Tbsp oyster sauce. Cover and simmer for 2 hours. Check occasionally. Add more water if needed.

Cooking Know-how

The reason for deboning the duck is so that you can then tuck the whole fowl into a pressure cooker. With bones intact, a duck is generally too long to fit into a standard pressure cooker.

Bean Curd Sticks and Gingko Nuts with Eggs
Cooking time: 2 hours • Serves 4

Bean curd sticks (*fu zhu/ fu chok*) 150 g, soaked until soft
Precooked gingko nuts 40
Rock sugar 150 g
Water 1 litre
Eggs 2

1. Cut soft bean curd sticks into 5-cm pieces. Wash and drain.

2. If precooked gingko nuts are unavailable, soak dried ones in water until soft. Remove skins and bitter cores if necessary.

3. Except eggs, combine all other ingredients in a pot. Simmer for 2 hours. Just before serving, crack eggs into a bowl and swirl into soup. Stir gently to break yolks. Serve hot or cold.

Opposite: Bean Curd Sticks and Gingko Nuts with Eggs.

Mutton Soup with Barley, Chinese Angelica and Wolfberries
Cooking time: 1-2 hours • Serves 4

Combining mutton and Chinese angelica promises to give much nourishment and 'warmth'. The hearty flavours here are tempered by the addition of barley and Chinese wolfberries, both of which are very subtle-tasting. Barley is, in fact, quite bland but acts as a foil for rich gravies, absorbing the incorporated flavours.

Mutton 450 g, cleaned and cut into large chunks

Chinese angelica (*dang gui/dong kwai*) 30 g, thinly sliced

Chinese wolfberries (*gou qi zi/gei chi*) 2 Tbsp

Barley 100 g, washed and drained

Water 1 litre

Salt 2 tsp

Ground black pepper ½ tsp

1. Combine all ingredients in a deep pot. Cover and simmer for 1–2 hours.

2. Add more liquid if necessary. Adjust to taste with seasoning. Serve piping hot for the smell of mutton is stronger when cold.

Euryale Seeds and Longan
Cooking time: 1 hour 30 minutes • Serves 4

The euryale seed looks like a small corn kernel but performs a strange feat when cooked. Each seed opens up into a little flower of sorts and has a texture and taste not unlike barley. This recipe makes a sweet soup that can be drunk at any time but is reputed to be good for ailments of the spleen and even gonorrhoea. It is also a variation of the longan tea so loved by the Straits Chinese, or Peranakan, community as a pre-meal drink. Served chilled, it is a light dessert with the euryale seeds providing lots of crunch.

Euryale seeds (*qian shi/ see sat*) 100 g, washed

Dried longan flesh 100 g, washed and thoroughly cleaned

Screwpine (*pandan*) **leaves** 2, washed and tied into a knot

Rock sugar 150 g

Water 1.5 litres

1. Combine all ingredients in a pot. Simmer over low heat for 1 hour 30 minutes.

Cooking Know-how

This recipe also can be prepared by pressure cooking for 45 minutes with 1 litre water. The amount of water added really depends on how light or rich you want the drink to be.

Opposite: Euryale Seeds and Longan.

Oxtail with Carrots and Eucommia Bark Cooking time: 2 hours • Serves 4

Eucommia bark is reputedly good for the kidneys, liver and ligaments. An unusual-looking ingredient, it gives a real boost to a dish already rich from the oxtail. The carrots and red dates add subtle sweetness.

Oxtail 700 g, cut into large chunks and excess fat and gristle trimmed

Large carrot 1, cut into chunks

Dried red dates (*hong zao/hung cho*) 10, pitted

Eucommia bark (*du zhong/dou chong*) 15 g

Salt 2 tsp

Water 2 litres

1. Combine all ingredients in a pot. Cover and simmer over low heat for about 2 hours or until flesh falls off the bone.

Double-cooked Pork with Apricot Kernels and Lotus Seeds Cooking time: 1 hour • Serves 4

Double-cooking pork is a favourite method of the northern Chinese. To first deep-fry the pork and then braise it achieves near-perfect texture and flavour. Deep-frying the pork acts to seal in flavour and also renders the pork skin a nice crunchy brown. The subsequent braising tenderises the meat fibres, and the cooked pork breaks apart into tasty shreds. This recipe uses both sweet and bitter apricot kernels, as well as lotus seeds for bulk. It is delicious with plain boiled or steamed rice.

Belly pork 1 piece, about 900 g

Dark soy sauce 2 Tbsp

Salt 2 tsp

Sweet apricot kernels (*nan xing/nam hung*) 10, washed and drained

Bitter apricot kernels (*bei xing/puk hung*) 10, washed and drained

Precooked lotus seeds 40, washed and drained

Water 1.5 litres

Cooking oil for deep-frying

1. Wash and dry belly pork. Make deep scores on the skin about 2 cm apart. Rub all over with soy sauce and salt. Set aside for 1 hour.

2. Heat oil for deep-frying. Fry pork for 2 minutes. Drain off as much oil as possible on kitchen paper.

3. Combine all ingredients in a deep casserole. Braise for about 1 hour. If the apricot kernels prove too bitter, adjust to taste with 1 tsp sugar. Serve with rice.

Opposite: Oxtail with Carrots and Eucommia Bark.

Chicken with Mushrooms and Chinese Wolfberries

Cooking time: 1 hour • Serves 4

A light and delicious soup that has a subtle sweetness from the Chinese wolfberries. Use trimmed and skinned chicken for optimum results.

Chicken 1, about 900 g

Dried Chinese mushrooms 8, soaked until soft and stalks discarded

Chinese wolfberries (*gou qi zi/gei chi*) 2 Tbsp

Water 1 litre

Salt 2 tsp

Ground black pepper ¹/₂ tsp

Fresh coriander (cilantro) leaves

1. Clean chicken thoroughly. Remove head, neck and feet. Do not use gizzard for this soup.

2. Except pepper and coriander, combine all other ingredients in a pot. Simmer for 1 hour. Serve with pepper and coriander.

Braised Belly Pork with Chestnuts and Chinese Wolfberries
Cooking time: 1 hour 30 minutes • Serves 4

The flavours of this dish make it rather similar to those of duck braised in soy sauce. Pork, however, is far less distinctive in taste than duck and also takes less time to cook. This dish is delicious when served with Chinese steamed buns (man tou/man tau) or plain steamed rice. Chinese wolfberries are famous for maintaining good eyesight.

Belly pork with skin on 900 g

Ground white pepper 1 tsp

Salt 2 tsp

Dark soy sauce 2 Tbsp

Cooking oil 3 Tbsp

Dried chestnuts 30, boiled and skins rubbed off

Chinese wolfberries (*gou qi zi/gei chi*) 2 Tbsp

Cinnamon stick 1, about 8-cm long

Star anise 2

Water 1.5 litres

1. Clean pork. Use a sharp knife to score the side of lean meat lengthways (lengthwise); score only as far as the lean meat extends. Pork piece should be divided into 2–3 strips, where each strip is about 3-cm wide. This facilitates slicing after cooking.

2. Rub prepared pork with pepper, salt and soy sauce. Let stand for 30 minutes.

3. Heat oil. Fry pork over high heat to singe and shrink. Remove and set aside. In remaining oil, fry prepared chestnuts, Chinese wolfberries, cinnamon stick and star anise for 2 minutes. Add water and pork. Cover and simmer for about 1 hour.

Cooking Know-how

This recipe can also be simmered in a pressure cooker. Reduce water to 750 ml and cook for 8–10 minutes at the pressure setting for meats. Do not overcook or chestnuts will disintegrate.

Opposite: Braised Belly Pork with Chestnuts and Chinese Wolfberries.

Dried Scallops, Brown Marrow and Pork Ribs
Cooking time: 1 hour • Serves 4

Although dried scallops are not quite in the category of herbal ingredients, they are nevertheless sold by medicinal shops and top quality ones can sometimes be worth their weight in gold. Brown pieces the size of marshmallows, dried scallops impart a beautiful flavour to whatever soup or stew you add them to.

Dried scallops (*gan bei/ kong yu chi*) 6, boiled until broken into shreds then drained
Large brown marrow 1, peeled, seeded and cut into 3-cm thick rings
Pork ribs 300 g, washed
Water 1.5 litres
Salt 2 tsp
Ground black pepper 1/2 tsp

1. Except pepper, combine all other ingredients in a pot. Simmer for about 1 hour. Serve hot with pepper.

Chicken Stuffed with Codonopsis Root
Cooking time: 2 hours • Serves 4

White in colour, this stew is eaten for its reputed efficacy gained from the codonopsis root. Slightly different from the standard double-boiled chicken dish, of which diners usually only drink the broth and toy with the chicken, this recipe utilises the slow-braising process that renders the chicken tender without robbing it of its flavour, and also produces a broth that is undeniably rich.

Chicken 1, about 900 g
Salt 2 tsp
Codonopsis root (*dang shen/dong sam*) 100 g
Water 1.5 litres

1. Clean chicken thoroughly, inside and out. Pat dry with kitchen paper. Rub with salt. Stuff cavity with codonopsis root. Place in a deep casserole. Add water.

2. Cover and braise over low heat for 2 hours. Check liquid level every 30 minutes or so. Add boiling water if necessary.

Cooking Know-how

This recipe can also be pressure cooked. In so doing, halve the amount of liquid used to 750 ml and also cooking time.

Opposite: Dried Scallops, Brown Marrow and Pork Ribs.

Dried Scallops and Pig's Tripe with Chinese Wolfberries

Cooking time: 2 hours • Serves 4

Most supermarkets sell precooked tripe that saves you bags of time. The recipe is for a very rich soup that, despite the inexpensive tripe, brooks no stinging on good ingredients like dried scallops. The soup is believed to restore Qi and also counter general malaise after childbirth.

Dried scallops (*gan bei/ kong yu chi*) 4, boiled until broken into shreds and drained

Precooked pig's tripe 450 g, washed and cut into bite-sized pieces

Chinese wolfberries (*gou qi zi/gei chi*) 2 Tbsp

Ground white pepper 2 tsp

Salt 2 tsp

Water 1 litre

1. Combine all ingredients in a pot. Simmer for 2 hours. Add liquid if necessary.

Cooking Know-how

Aside from stove-top simmering, this recipe can also be double-boiled or pressure cooked. Double-boiling will take about 3 hours, while pressure cooking shortens cooking time to 1 hour. Also, halve the specified amount of water to 500 ml if pressure cooking.

Duck with Chinese Honeyed Dates and Tangerine Peel

Cooking time: 2 hours • Serves 4

Not frequently used in savoury cooking, Chinese honeyed dates are, as the name implies, dates preserved in honey. With poultry like duck, however, a touch of sweetness from the dates and the zest of tangerine peel works to temper the bird's rich oiliness, much like how orange does in the classic French duck l'orange. Here, the different flavours blend beautifully after prolonged slow cooking.

Duck 1, about 1.5 kg

Chinese honeyed dates (*mi zao/mutt cho*) 4

Dried tangerine peel 3 pieces

Salt 2 tsp

Water 2 litres

1. Clean duck thoroughly. Cut into large joints. Remove every bit of skin and fat from the regions of the neck and breast. Remove parson's nose, especially the glands on either side.

2. Combine all ingredients in a pot. Simmer for about 2 hours. At the end of cooking time, liquid in the pot should have halved.

Cooking Know-how

This recipe can be pressure cooked, which means that the amount of water can be reduced by as much as half, as long as all of the duck joints are covered by liquid.

Opposite: Duck with Chinese Honeyed Dates and Tangerine Peel.

Mushrooms with Chestnuts and Lily Bulb Petals
Cooking time: 1 hour • Serves 4

A richer and more nourishing version of the classic Cantonese braised mushrooms, this dish is much more substantial with the addition of chestnuts. Imparting fragrance and lightness to the dish, lily bulb petals balance the richness of the mushrooms and chestnuts. Sometimes, lettuce is used in place of chestnuts.

Dried Chinese mushrooms 20, soaked until soft and with stalks discarded

Dried chestnuts 20, boiled for 10 minutes, with skins rubbed off when cooled, then washed and drained

Dried lily bulb petals (*bai he/bak hup*) 15 g

Belly pork 1 piece, about 100 g

Oyster sauce 2 Tbsp

Water 750 ml

Sugar 1 tsp

Salt 1 tsp

1. Combine all ingredients in a non-stick pot or casserole. Add enough water to completely cover ingredients. Simmer for 1 hour. Add water if necessary.

Cooking Know-how

If you dislike the fatty taste of belly pork, substitute with a tablespoon of corn or peanut oil.

Duck with Chinese Angelica and Wine
Cooking time: 2-3 hours • Serves 4

Some believe that the richness of duck should be tempered with a stuffing of some kind, but in this case, the Chinese angelica and rose wine form a formidable combination in counteracting the flavourful effects of the duck. When buying duck, choose one that has the least fat around the nose area and remember to remove this extremity.

Duck 1, about 2 kg

Dark soy sauce 3 Tbsp

Salt 2 tsp

Chinese angelica (*dang gui/dong kwai*) 60 g

Chinese rose wine (*mei gui lu/mui gwai lo*) 2 Tbsp

Ground white pepper 1 tsp

Sugar 2 tsp

Water 1.5 litres

1. Clean duck thoroughly. Pat dry with kitchen paper. Rub all over with dark soy sauce and salt.

2. Heat a dry non-stick wok. Singe duck all over until skin is brown and taut. Transfer to a deep pot.

3. Add all remaining ingredients. Bring to the boil. Cover and simmer for 2–3 hours.

4. Before serving, skim off as much fat as you can from the surface.

Cooking Know-how

Chinese rose wine is, as the name suggests, a wine infused with rose essence or extract and is absolutely delicious when used in conjunction with meat or poultry.

Opposite: Mushrooms with Chestnuts and Lily Bulb Petals.

Steamed Winter Melon with Crabmeat, Chestnuts, Lotus Seeds and Barley Cooking time: 2 hours • Serves 4

Here is a rich change from the simple winter melon soup commonly served at the end of a Chinese banquet. Dried scallops were included in this recipe purely for added flavour, while crab in the recipe can be replaced with other shellfish if desired. Regard winter melon as a blank canvas and create your own masterpiece.

Winter melon 1 whole, about 1.5 kg

Dried scallops (*gan bei/ kong yu chi*) 3

Fresh crabmeat 200 g

Dried lotus seeds 20, boiled, cored and with skins rubbed off

Dried chestnuts 20, boiled, cored and with skins rubbed off

Barley 4 Tbsp

Salt 2 tsp

Ground white pepper 1 tsp

1. Peel winter melon. Slice off about three-eighths from one end. At the other end, slice off just enough so melon can sit on a plate without wobbling. Remove melon seeds. Scoop out enough melon flesh to leave about 2-cm thickness throughout. Be careful not to make a hole.

2. Boil dried scallops in 200 ml water for 15 minutes. Drain scallop pieces. Reserve stock.

3. Combine all ingredients in a container. Add enough scallop stock to thoroughly moisten all ingredients.

4. Tightly pack combined ingredients into melon bowl. With open end facing up, place melon bowl on a plate. Steam for 2 hours.

5. When done, place a serving plate over melon. Very carefully turn over. What you have will be a pale winter melon sphere cupped over its stuffing.

6. To serve, bring melon sphere to the table. Cut down along its side to reveal the gems of your creation. You will be admired for your culinary skills.

Chicken with Ginseng and Lotus Root Soup

Cooking time: 1 hour • Serves 4

This parent stem of the famous lotus seeds has a peculiar and unique texture and taste. Cantonese cooks treat lotus root in many ways, one of which is to deep-fry slices of the root and then fill the holes with glutinous rice.

Chicken 1, about 700 g

Ginseng 20 g

Lotus root 300 g, thoroughly cleaned and diagonally cut into 1-cm thick slices

Water 1 litre

Salt 2 tsp

Ground white pepper 1 tsp

1. Combine all ingredients in a pot. Simmer for 1 hour.

Cooking Know-how

If you have a slight distaste for lotus root, then it is most likely caused by the minute amount of sap that clings to the root. The effect of the sap, however, vanishes if slices of the root are thoroughly cooked through. Another way to ensure the sap's removal is to blanch slices of the root in plenty of boiling water for several minutes prior to cooking and then drain.

Opposite: Chicken with Ginseng and Lotus Root Soup.

Chicken Broth with Barley, Euryale and Lotus Seeds

Cooking time: 1 hour • Serves 4

Here is a rich change from the simple winter melon soup commonly served at the end of a Chinese banquet. Dried scallops were included in this recipe purely for added flavour, while crab in the recipe can be replaced with other shellfish if desired. Regard winter melon as a blank canvas and create your own masterpiece.

Chicken 1, about 900 g
Barley 3 Tbsp, washed
Euryale seeds (*qian shi/see sat*) 15 g, washed
Precooked lotus seeds 40, washed
Water 1 litre
Salt 2 tsp
Ground white pepper 1/2 tsp

1. Clean chicken thoroughly. Remove head and feet. Leave whole.

2. Combine all ingredients in a pot. Simmer for 1 hour or until chicken is fork-tender.

Chicken with Gingko Nuts, Lotus Seeds and Chinese Wolfberries
Cooking time: 1 hour 30 minutes • Serves 4

I have experimented with duck, pork and chicken for this recipe and recommend the lattermost as the perfect foil for the rich compote of ingredients and redolent gravy. The work of Chinese wine and wolfberries give this dish its wonderful flavour.

Chicken 1, about 900 g
Dark soy sauce 2 Tbsp
Salt 1 tsp
Cooking oil 2 Tbsp
Chinese wolfberries (*gou qi zi/gei chi*) 2 Tbsp
Chinese cooking wine (*hua diao/fa diew*) 2 Tbsp
Oyster sauce 2 Tbsp
Ground white pepper 1 tsp
Salt 1 tsp
Water 1 litre
Precooked gingko nuts 40
Precooked lotus seeds 40

1. Clean chicken thoroughly. Rub all over with dark soy sauce and salt. Let stand for 30 minutes.

2. Heat oil. Fry chicken over high heat until skin is brown. Remove and drain.

3. Transfer remaining oil to a large, glazed clay pot with a snug-fitting lid. Fry wolfberries for 1–2 minutes. Add all seasonings and water. Bring to the boil. Add fried chicken. Simmer over low heat for 40 minutes. Turn once or twice so the chicken's thick parts cook through.

4. Add gingko nuts and lotus seeds. Simmer for 15 minutes more. If gravy seems pale, add 1 Tbsp dark soy sauce. Adjust to taste with a dash of oyster sauce or more salt if desired.

Opposite: Chicken with Gingko Nuts, Lotus Seeds and Chinese Wolfberries.

Mixed Meat Hotpot with Lotus Seeds and Chrysanthemum Cooking time: 1 hour • Serves 4

This is a lovely variation of the standard steamboat, with beef, mutton and chicken slices perfumed by chrysanthemum petals. It can also be served steamboat style with all the ingredients assembled for guests to individually select and, in the process, create their own flavours. Lotus seeds and chrysanthemum combine to make a very potent 'cooling' agent.

Beef fillet 200 g, thinly sliced

Lean mutton 200 g, thinly sliced

Skinned chicken breasts 2, thinly sliced

Precooked lotus seeds 30

Water or stock 2 litres

Dried chrysanthemum petals 30 g

Salt 2 tsp or more to taste

Ground white pepper to taste

1. Arrange beef, mutton and chicken slices on separate plates. Then, arrange plates around steamboat or fondue pot at table's centre. Divide lotus seeds into several bowls to be placed around the table.

2. Bring water or stock to the boil. Steep dried chrysanthemum for 15 minutes, then strain and discard. Add salt.

3. Guests may now do their own cooking and seasoning at the table. The soup at the end of the meal will be very rich, and you can temper it by tossing in vegetables like thinly sliced Chinese cabbage.

Beef and Yam with Ginseng, Chinese Yam and Wolfberries Cooking time: 1 hour 30 minutes • Serves 4

This dish will stoke the fires of a flagging system. A 'warming' and substantial dish, it helps to restore the body's 'heat'. Add a handful of Chinese mushrooms for a smoky flavour.

Sirloin steak 700 g, cut into large chunks

Chinese yam (*shan yao/ wai san*) 15 g, rinsed and drained

Chinese wolfberries (*gou qi zi/gei chi*) 1 Tbsp, rinsed and drained

Water 1.5 litres

Salt 2 tsp

Yam 200 g, peeled and cut into large chunks

1. Except yam, combine all other ingredients in a pot. Bring to the boil. Lower heat. Simmer for 1 hour.

2. Add yam. Simmer for 30 minutes more. The yam pieces will render the gravy quite thick.

Opposite: Beef and Yam with Ginseng, Chinese Yam and Wolfberries.

Fish with Cordyceps and Chinese Wolfberries

Cooking time: 1 hour • Serves 4

Fish is one ingredient that does not feature frequently in Chinese herbal cooking but is, nevertheless, touted as being beneficial to liver and kidney functions when combined with cordyceps. Chinese wolfberries are known for their efficacy in improving eyesight. The best kinds of fish to use are those species that have firm, relatively boneless meat. Garoupa and threadfin are recommended for this hearty soup.

Garoupa or threadfin
450 g
Cordyceps (*dong chong xia cao/dong chong cho*)
15 g, rinsed
Chinese wolfberries (*gou qi zi/gei chi*)
1 Tbsp, rinsed
Water 800 ml
Chinese cooking wine (*hua diao/fa dew*) 3 Tbsp
Salt 2 tsp

1. Cut off fish head. Make several deep cuts along the body, almost to the bone. Leave large, central bone intact but remove as many small bones as possible. Wash and drain thoroughly.

2. Combine rinsed ingredients and water in a pot. Cover and simmer for 40 minutes. When done, volume should be reduced to about three quarters. Remove from heat.

3. Add fish, wine and salt. Jiggle pot a little to incorporate. Cover and simmer for 15 minutes more.

Abalone and Chicken with Chinese Yam   Cooking time: 1 hour • Serves 4

This is a dish fit for emperors, and it pays to use the best abalone you can afford. The chicken, even when skinned, provides enough fat to give the dish a 'smoothness' the Cantonese appreciate, as reflected in their term for it — wat. Chinese yam is a tonic for kidneys and lungs and, at the same time, aids urinary functions. Canned abalone is perfectly acceptable as dried ones take forever to process.

Precooked abalone 300 g, thinly sliced
Skinned chicken 1, about 900 g
Chinese yam (*shan yao/ wai san*) 10 slivers
Water 1 litre
Salt 2 tsp
Ground black pepper 1 tsp

1. Lightly tenderise abalone slices with blunt edge of a cleaver. Wash and drain slices.

2. Clean chicken. Leave whole or cut into 4 large joints.

3. Place Chinese yam in a pot. Add all other ingredients over the top. Cover and simmer over low–medium heat for 1 hour. Check occasionally to see if more liquid needs to be added.

4. When done, the chicken should fall off the bone, and abalone just tender enough.

Opposite: Fish with Cordyceps and Chinese Wolfberries.

Buddha's Feast Cooking time: 1 hour • Serves 8

Better known to the Chinese as luo han zai in Mandarin or lor hawn chai in Cantonese, this is a favourite festive dish. The recipe requires a lot of pre-cooking preparation, but the flavours that blend so beautifully and emerge the day after it is cooked, which is incidentally the best time to serve it, makes it all worthwhile. If you cannot get all the ingredients listed here, modify as you please without cutting down too much on the number of ingredients. Traditionally, it should contain 18 different ingredients, each symbolic of the 18 luo han or disciples of Buddha.

Do not confuse sweetened bean curd wafers, also known as teem chok in Cantonese, with bean curd sticks, or fu chok. The former are perfectly rectangular, wafer-sized, coffee-coloured pieces, while the latter are irregularly shaped, pale-yellow sticks.

Precooked gingko nuts 40, washed and thoroughly drained, as well as cored if necessary

Precooked lotus seeds 40, washed and thoroughly drained, as well as cored if necessary

Dried Chinese mushrooms 12, soaked until soft and stalks discarded

Chinese cabbage 300 g, cut into 5-cm long pieces, washed and drained

Sweetened bean curd wafers (*tian zhu/teem chok*) 4, cut into 5-cm long pieces, soaked until soft and drained

Dried lily buds (golden needles) 100 g, soaked until soft, each tied into a firm knot and with hard tips cut off

Dried red dates (*hong zao/hung cho*) 20, pitted and washed

Cloud ear fungus (*yun er/wun yi*) 3 Tbsp, soaked until soft, washed and drained

Canned button mushrooms 200 g, drained

Canned straw mushrooms 200 g, drained

Transparent vermicelli (*fen si/fun see*) 60 g, soaked until soft

Black hair moss (*fa cai/fat choy*) 15 g, soaked, thoroughly cleaned and drained

Ginger 1 large knob, about 60 g

Preserved red bean curd (*nan ru/nam yu*) 4–6 pieces

Hoisin sauce 3 Tbsp

Oyster sauce 3 Tbsp

Sugar 1 Tbsp

Water 2 litres

Cooking oil for deep-frying

1. The traditional way of preparing this dish involved separately deep-frying all the ingredients, except the mushrooms, vermicelli, black hair moss and seasonings, in a wok of hot oil. This step, however, can be eliminated if you do not like the dish oily.

2. If you chose to deep-fry, remove bulk of oil until 3 Tbsp remain. Bruise ginger with skin on. Add to wok. Fry ginger until fragrant, then push aside. Add preserved red bean curd. Mash with spatula and sauté quickly.

3. Except sugar and water, add all other ingredients. Toss thoroughly. When well mixed, add sugar and water. Cover and simmer for about 1 hour.

4. Adjust to taste by adding more preserved bean curd (for saltiness), hoisin sauce (for flavour) and/or oyster sauce (for richness). Do not add any salt. Add water if necessary. Consistency should be that of a thick stew.

Cooking Know-how

To deep-fry successfully, the oil has to be smoking hot and the ingredients to be fried have to be completely dry. Place only one ingredient on a wire ladle before lowering into hot oil. When done, drain.

Chicken with Chestnuts and Chinese Wolfberries

Cooking time: 1 hour • Serves 4

For this dish, use a larger than normal chicken as anything less is likely to break up after long stewing or braising.

Chicken 1, about 1.5 kg

Dark soy sauce 2 Tbsp

Salt 3 tsp

Cooking oil 4 Tbsp

Dried chestnuts 30, boiled for 15 minutes, with skins rubbed off when cooled, then washed and drained

Chinese wolfberries (*gou qi zi/gei chi*) 1 Tbsp

Oyster sauce 3 Tbsp

Ground white pepper 1 tsp

Water 1.5 litres

Iceberg lettuce 1 head

1. Clean chicken thoroughly. Leave head and neck intact. Drain. Rub all over with dark soy sauce and 1 tsp salt. Let stand for 15 minutes.

2. Heat oil. Fry chicken over high heat. Remove when well browned all over. Leave to cool.

3. In remaining oil, fry chestnuts for 3 minutes.

4. Add remaining salt, wolfberries, oyster sauce, pepper, and a few Tbsp water. When mixture is almost dry, remove and stuff into chicken. Sew up with thread to seal cavity. Place in a deep casserole. Arrange excess stuffing around the chicken to be cooked together.

5. Pour remaining water over chicken. Cover and simmer for about 1 hour. Add water if necessary. Adjust to taste with 1–2 Tbsp oyster sauce. Be mindful that flavour from the stuffing will eventually seep out and blend with braising liquid.

6. If chicken seems underdone, simmer for 30 minutes more. Serve on a bed of lettuce. Leave extra liquid on the side for anyone who likes to mix it with rice.

Dried Scallops, Lotus Seeds and Chinese Angelica in Winter Melon
Cooking time: 2 hours • Serves 4

There is simply a variation of the previous recipe with Chinese angelica as the backbone of nourishment. A soupy dish, the winter melon here becomes more like a receptacle. The melon and its contents are steamed in a large steamer with a high, dome-shaped lid. The result is regarded as an extremely nourishing soup, especially for invalids and new mothers.

Dried scallops (*gan bei/ kong yu chi*) 4–5

Winter melon 1 whole, about 1.5 kg

Precooked lotus seeds 20

Chinese angelica (*dang gui/dong kwai*) 20 g

Water 600 ml

Salt 2 tsp

1. Boil scallops in some water. Drain scallop pieces. Shred if necessary. Reserve stock.

2. Cut off top of winter melon. Remove seeds. Scoop out excess flesh until a pot-shaped receptacle remains.

3. Fill melon bowl with all ingredients. Add scallop stock and as much water as the melon can hold. Place melon on a deep plate. Steam for 2 hours.

Opposite: Dried Scallops, Lotus Seeds and Chinese Angelica in Winter Melon.

Weights and Measures

Quantities for this book are given in Metric and American (spoon) measures. Standard spoon and cup measurements used are: 1 teaspoon = 5 ml, 1 tablespoon = 15 ml, 1 cup = 250 ml. All measures are level unless otherwise stated.

Liquid & Volume Measures

Metric	Imperial	American
5 ml	$^1/_6$ fl oz	1 teaspoon
10 ml	$^1/_3$ fl oz	1 dessertspoon
15 ml	$^1/_2$ fl oz	1 tablespoon
60 ml	2 fl oz	$^1/_4$ cup (4 tablespoons)
85 ml	$2^1/_2$ fl oz	$^1/_3$ cup
90 ml	3 fl oz	$^3/_8$ cup (6 tablespoons)
125 ml	4 fl oz	$^1/_2$ cup
180 ml	6 fl oz	$^3/_4$ cup
250 ml	8 fl oz	1 cup
300 ml	10 fl oz ($^1/_2$ pint)	$1^1/_4$ cups
375 ml	12 fl oz	$1^1/_2$ cups
435 ml	14 fl oz	$1^3/_4$ cups
500 ml	16 fl oz	2 cups
625 ml	20 fl oz (1 pint)	$2^1/_2$ cups
750 ml	24 fl oz	3 cups
1 litre	32 fl oz	4 cups
1.25 litres	40 fl oz (2 pints)	5 cups
1.5 litres	48 fl oz	6 cups
2.5 litres	80 fl oz (4 pints)	10 cups

Dry Measures

Metric	Imperial
30 grams	1 ounce
45 grams	$1^1/_2$ ounces
55 grams	2 ounces
70 grams	$2^1/_2$ ounces
85 grams	3 ounces
100 grams	$3^1/_2$ ounces
110 grams	4 ounces
125 grams	$4^1/_2$ ounces
140 grams	5 ounces
280 grams	10 ounces
450 grams	16 ounces, 1 pound
500 grams	1 pound, $1^1/_2$ ounces
700 grams	$1^1/_2$ pounds
800 grams	$1^3/_4$ pounds
1 kilogram	2 pounds, 3 ounces
1.5 kilograms	3 pounds, $4^1/_2$ ounces
2 kilograms	4 pounds, 6 ounces

Oven Temperature

	°C	°F	Gas Regulo
Very slow	120	250	1
Slow	150	300	2
Moderately slow	160	325	3
Moderate	180	350	4
Moderately hot	190/200	375/400	5/6
Hot	210/220	410/425	6/7
Very hot	230	450	8
Super hot	250/290	475/550	9/10

Length

Metric	Imperial
0.5 cm	$^1/_4$ inch
1 cm	$^1/_2$ inch
1.5 cm	$^3/_4$ inch
2.5 cm	1 inch